The California Frog-Jumping Contest

Algebra

Bill Jacob

Catherine Twomey Fosnot

Heinemann
361 Hanover St.
Portsmouth, NH 03801
www.heinemann.com

Houghton Mifflin Harcourt
222 Berkeley Street
Boston, MA 02116
www.hmhco.com

Offices and agents throughout the world

ISBN 13: 978-0-325-01024-3
ISBN 10: 0-325-01024-2

ISBN 13: 978-0-15-360576-5
ISBN 10: 0-15-360576-6

"Dedicated to Teachers" is a trademark of
Greenwood Publishing Group, Inc.

The development of a portion of the material described within was supported in part
by the National Science Foundation under Grant No. 9911841. Any opinions, findings,
and conclusions or recommendations expressed in these materials are those of the
authors and do not necessarily reflect the views of the National Science Foundation.

Library of Congress Cataloging-in-Publication Data
CIP data is on file with the Library of Congress

Printed in the United States of America on acid-free paper

20 19 18 17   EBM   1 2 3 4

Acknowledgements

Photography

Herbert Seignoret
Mathematics in the City, City College of New York

Illustrator

T. Kyle Gentry

Schools featured in photographs

The Muscota New School/PS 314 (an empowerment school in Region 10), New York, NY
Independence School/PS 234 (Region 9), New York, NY
Fort River Elementary School, Amherst, MA

Contents

Unit Overview

This unit uses the context of the famous short story by Mark Twain—*The Celebrated Jumping Frog of Calaveras County*—to develop equivalence and its use in solving algebraic problems. The context of a frog jumping along a track is used to foster number line representations in which students solve for an unknown amount, which is usually the length of a frog jump. Equivalent sequences of jumps are represented naturally on a double number line by having them start and end at the same location, with one expression shown on top of the line and the other shown underneath the line. The representation can then be used as a tool for solving the problem.

The unit begins with a problem in which students find the length of a bullfrog's jump, knowing the full length of a sequence of his jumps and steps. This context leads to using the number line as a tool for solving problems with unknowns. Next, students must find various approaches for lining up six- or eight-foot benches for two jumping tracks of lengths 28 and 42 feet. Students utilize the equivalence $6 + 6 + 6 + 6 = 8 + 8 + 8$ to change one

The Landscape of Learning

BIG IDEAS

- ☀ An algebraic expression can be treated as an object (not only as a procedure)
- ☀ Variation: variables describe relationships and are not merely unknown quantities
- ☀ Equivalence: algebraic expressions can appear different yet be equivalent objects
- ☀ Equivalent expressions can be used interchangeably
- ☀ Equivalent amounts can be separated off
- ☀ Equivalent expressions can be operated on, by $+$ or $-$, $\times$ and $\div$, to give new equivalencies

STRATEGIES

- ☀ Guessing and checking
- ☀ Guessing, checking, and adjusting based on the result
- ☀ Using equivalence to separate off equal amounts
- ☀ Using equivalence or amounts of change to remove a variable
- ☀ Symbolizing with variables
- ☀ Justifying by doing several problems
- ☀ Justifying by explaining why
- ☀ Proving with all possible cases

MODELS

- ☀ Double open number line
- ☀ Combination chart

possible solution into a second possible solution and use the number line to represent this equivalence. A similar problem about fences is used to develop a combination chart, which is a useful representation for determining net gain (or loss) after an exchange.

The second half of the unit includes more frog-jumping problems as the frogs plan for their Olympic Games. Now students further explore the use of variables to represent more complex situations and solve for unknown amounts. Here, students use the number line to represent jumps in the problems, and can separate off equal amounts of unknown lengths to determine the lengths of unknown amounts. As the unit progresses, the questions require that students investigate equivalent lengths of different-sized jumps, and work with these equivalences flexibly to solve problems.

The complexity of learning to symbolize has been the subject of extensive research. One study, summarized in *Adding It Up* (National Research Council 2001, 264), illustrates typical difficulties students may have. One such difficulty, known as the reversal error, is illustrated by work on the following problem: *At a certain university, there are six times as many students as professors. Using* s *for the number of students and* p *for the number of professors, write an equation that gives the relation between the number of students and the number of professors.* A majority of students, ranging from first-year algebra students to college freshmen, wrote the equation $6s = p$. Apparently they used 6 as an adjective and s as a noun, following the natural language in the problem. However, they needed to multiply the number of professors by 6 to find the number of students. The correct response is $6p = s$. Because learning to write algebraic expressions is so difficult, we don't push symbolizing early in this unit. The representation of the number line is used to fix students' attention on the distinction between the lengths of jumps and the number of jumps. Once this is set, students can begin symbolizing in problems like this in a meaningful way. The unit ends with the students constructing more formal algebraic notation as they develop methods to simplify their earlier representations.

The Mathematical Landscape

What is algebra and how does understanding of it develop? Algebra has many aspects, for example, generalizing beyond specific instances; describing and representing patterns and functions; building equations and expressions using symbolic representations with integers and variables; and manipulating symbols to simplify equations, prove relations, and solve for unknowns.

From 2003 to 2006, several mathematicians, researchers, and teachers participated in a think tank at Mathematics in the City to explore several questions:

✦ What might algebra look like as it emerges in the elementary years?

✦ What are some of the critical big ideas and strategies young learners construct that might serve as important landmarks for teachers to notice, develop, and celebrate?

✦ How might realistic contexts and models support such development?

To answer these questions, we designed instructional sequences and field-tested many activities. This unit and *Trades, Jumps, and Stops*, also in the *Contexts for Learning Mathematics* series, are a result of the work we did together.

The most commonly employed models and manipulatives for algebra are balance pans and algebra tiles. But researchers have found these to have serious drawbacks: students do not always have a deep enough understanding of conservation of weight for the balance pan model to make sense (Piaget 1954), and the use of tiles may produce a passive "reading off" behavior rather than cognitive involvement in the actions undertaken.

In our previous work on number and operation (addressed in many of the other units in the *Contexts for Learning Mathematics* series), we used the open number line model. Because our algebra work was an extension of our work with number and operation, we began to explore the use of the open number line as a model for algebra as well. In the study of number and operation, the open number line aligns better than base-ten blocks with students' invented strategies for addition and subtraction, and it stimulates a mental representation of numbers and number operations that is more powerful for developing mental arithmetic strategies. Additionally, students using the open number line are cognitively involved in their actions (Klein, Beishuizen, and Treffers 2002). In our research on the development of algebra, we found that the open number line was a powerful model as well (Fosnot and Jacob, in preparation).

In contrast to a number line with counting numbers written below, an "open" number line is just an empty line used to record student's computation strategies. Only the numbers used and the operations are recorded as leaps or jumps. For example, if a child's strategy for adding $8 + 79$ is $79 + 1 + 7$, using a landmark number of 80, it can be recorded like this:

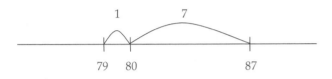

As we researched the development of big ideas and strategies in the algebra strand, we used a double open number line, with one expression represented above the line and the other represented underneath, to build an understanding of equations. The figure below represents the equation $9 + 5 = 8 + 6$:

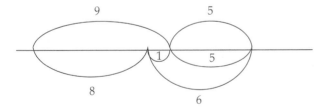

Instead of initially introducing algebraic notation with letters representing variables, the investigations in this unit are set in contexts in which varying quantities can be represented in ways that reflect the context and features of the quantity. The contexts selected for this unit lead naturally to representations on an open number line. If a frog takes three jumps and two steps, it is natural to represent its path as follows:

If the three jumps are understood as equal amounts and if the two steps are understood as equal amounts, then this figure can be understood as representing $3j + 2s$, where j represents the length of a jump and s represents the length of a step. If the step length is considered the "unit"—that is, a step length is 1—then the number line representation also can be understood as $3j + 2$, where j represents the length of a jump.

Students working through this unit might not write expressions such as $3j + 2$ until the end of the unit. Instead, they will work with representations such as these jumps on an open number line. These representations are important for several reasons. First, the representation gives meaning to expressions like $3j + 2$ even if the length of the jump is unknown. It is natural to consider adding the jumps and the steps (they add up to distance traveled), and now $3j + 2$ has a visual interpretation, as an object in itself. Second, the representations become a *tool* for problem solving. By combining representations according to the problem statement and context, students can consider the relationships between variables as spatial relations.

In this unit, the double number line is introduced as a way to mathematize a frog-jumping scenario with variables used to represent the lengths of the frog jumps. The double number line is also used as a tool for solving for unknowns and for representing relationships between expressions. For example, consider the jumping situation of a frog named Sunny. When he jumps 4 times and takes 11 steps, he is at the same point as when he jumps 5 times and takes 4 steps ($4j + 11 = 5j + 4$). What is the length of his jump? These jumps and steps can be represented on a double number line:

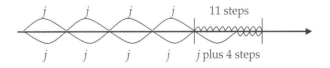

A representation like this is helpful in realizing that 11 steps is equivalent to 1 jump plus 4 steps. So the jump must be equal to 7 steps.

One difficulty that may arise early with this representation is that students will represent equivalence (3 jumps and 2 steps is equivalent to 4 jumps minus 6 steps, for example) on separate lines and then have trouble getting them to fit together on the same line because their representations have different lengths. This means they will have to redraw the representation to get it to fit the situation. Getting into difficulties and working through them is very important! The process of redrawing will model the fact that the jump is a variable quantity in the way the problem is posed, and the equivalence requires that it take on a particular value, which is represented in the redrawing. Look for moments of puzzlement like this. Don't hesitate to let students discuss their ideas, and be puzzled for short periods of time. This is when they construct new ideas. Then, celebrate their accomplishments!

BIG IDEAS

This unit is designed to encourage the development of some of the big ideas related to early algebra:

❖ *an algebraic expression can be treated as an object (not only as a procedure)*

❖ *variation: variables describe relationships and are not merely unknown quantities*

❖ *equivalence: algebraic expressions can appear different yet be equivalent objects*

❖ *equivalent expressions can be used interchangeably*

❖ *equivalent amounts can be separated off*

❖ *equivalent expressions can be operated on, by + or −, × and ÷, to give new equivalencies*

❖ An algebraic expression can be treated as an object (not only as a procedure)

Research has shown that many students comfortable with $x + 3 = 8$ do not understand how to interpret the expression $x + 3$ as an object by itself (National Research Council 2001). The confusion may be that they don't know how to combine the x and the 3, or that they believe that every time they add two things

the result has to equal something else. Yet often, in algebra, mathematicians want to work with expressions (like $x + 3$) in a meaningful way. In other words, they want to treat the expression *as an object.* Young students find it natural to solve for unknowns in equations. Even in first grade, students can think about questions like __ $+ 3 = 8$ and determine how to fill in the blank. Later, teachers may write $x + 3 = 8$ and tell the students "to find x" and again most students find this easy to think about. They just consider the question as what number is eight three more than, and then write $x = 5$. Here students see the use of the variable to represent an unknown value, and then by writing $x + 3 = 8$ they understand $x + 3$ in this context as an expression *to describe a procedure.* Even though students adapt easily to this usage, algebra remains a major hurdle for many; while studying algebra, many students learn to hate math or give up their aspirations to attend college. This has led educators around the world to wonder what is going wrong. While we don't have a complete answer, it seems clear that simply viewing algebra as the business of using variables to represent unknown values and using expressions to describe a procedure is inadequate.

One approach has been to teach students formal rules to indicate how to manipulate expressions, but we don't do that in this unit because we believe it doesn't help students construct this idea. Instead, we ask students to work with the context of frog jumps, where an expression such as *four jumps and eight steps* has meaning in and of itself and where an expression like this one can be compared to others on the open number line.

❖ Variation: Variables describe relationships and are not merely unknown quantities

In order to make sense of algebraic equations such as $x + 3 = y - 2$, students need to construct the idea of variation: the understanding that an indeterminate amount can be related to another indeterminate amount, and this relationship is meaningful even if the amounts are not known. This unit provides multiple contexts to support the development of this idea, such as a frog that jumps once and takes three steps forward landing at the same point as another frog that takes one jump and two steps backward.

The unit also provides an investigation involving lining the frog-jumping track, using six-foot and eight-foot benches along a 42-foot and a 28-foot track. Here the relationships $6 \times a + 8 \times b = 42$ and $6 \times c + 8 \times d = 28$ describe the relationship between the (unknown) numbers of benches of these two lengths.

❖ Equivalence: Algebraic expressions can appear different yet be equivalent objects

While investigating multiple solutions to problems such as finding different combinations of six-foot and eight-foot benches that add up to 42 feet or 28 feet, students construct the notion of equivalence in the context of variation. The 42-foot bench can be built with seven 6-foot benches or with three 6-foot benches and three 8-foot benches. Here, seven benches appear different than six benches; however, they are understood as being "equivalent" because they have the same overall length. This happens often in mathematics: objects that are different are thought of as being "the same" because of the context in which they are situated and the problem that is being solved. The subtlety is that perhaps in a different context they might not be viewed as the "same," and students must construct this distinction as part of the mathematizing and making sense of the context. The forms of equivalence increase in sophistication as the unit progresses. The first equivalent relationships students encounter with the benches are numerical: $6 + 6 + 6 + 6 = 8 + 8 + 8$. Later, students consider equivalent amounts involving a single unknown frog jump, such as when a frog taking 4 jumps and 11 steps lands in the same place as a frog taking 5 jumps and 4 steps. Eventually, students consider equivalent amounts of two proportionally related unknowns or equivalent amounts of two linearly related unknowns (systems).

❖ Equivalent expressions can be used interchangeably

For a student to understand an equation such as $6 \times a + 8 \times b = 42$ in the bench context, each expression on either side of the equation has to have meaning as an object, and the equivalence has to be understood as the overall length of benches, the number and type of which may vary. Once these ideas are constructed, students generalize the idea that as long as the objects are equivalent (3×8 feet $= 4 \times 6$ feet), they can be exchanged and the overall equality will still hold.

❖ Equivalent amounts can be separated off

To simplify an equation, mathematicians eliminate equivalent amounts. While this technique may seem obvious to adult mathematicians, young learners often feel the need initially to separate but keep equivalent amounts in a sort of "storage box" while they examine the pieces remaining. For example, consider the case of the frog, Sunny, who completes two trials: 4 jumps and 11 steps is the result of the first trial, and 5 jumps and 4 steps is the result of the second. Each time he lands in the same place at the end ($4j + 11 = 5j + 4$). In frog-jumping contests, referees assume that all jumps made by a particular frog are equal and all steps are considered equal, so these trials must be compared to determine the length of Sunny's jump in the competition. A mathematizing of this situation is represented on the number line:

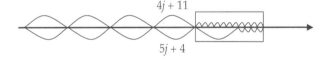

Since the four jumps in each trial are equivalent, the equation can be replaced with the equivalence of 11 steps with 1 jump and 4 steps. Only the boxed section needs to be examined, $11 = j + 4$. In a typical algebra course this process is sometimes referred to as "canceling," but you will probably find that your students will describe and conceptualize it differently. We have found that students do not like to use terms such as "canceling" (Fosnot and Jacob, in preparation), apparently because they do not like to throw the information away. Instead, they use terminology like "separating" or "putting it in a storage box." Recognizing that equal amounts can be separated, and that the remaining pieces are still equivalent requires an examination of the part-whole relations of the expressions and thus is a big idea for students.

❖ Equivalent expressions can be operated on by + or −, x and ÷, to give new equivalencies

Once expressions are understood as objects and equations are understood as an expression of the relationship between them, the big idea on the horizon is that whatever you do to one expression you must do to the other to maintain equivalence. In *Trades, Jumps, and Stops,* an early algebra unit in the *Contexts for Learning Mathematics* series, addition and subtraction are explored. This unit extends this idea to include the generalization that equivalent amounts can be used interchangeably in multiplication and division. For example, by removing equivalent amounts (in this case $x + x + x$) students can simplify relationships such as $x + x + x + 6 = x + x + x + x − 2$ into $6 = x − 2$. Later they work with systems of linear equivalences of the form $3x + y = 40$ and $4x + 2y = 58$. By subtracting equivalent expressions (in this case $4x + 2y − (3x + y)$ and $58 − 40$), the problem is simplified to $x + y = 18$. Multiplication and division can also be used. For example, if $4j + 8 = 52$, then $8j + 16 = 104$, or if $3j + 6 = 39$ then $6j + 12 = 78$, and $j + 2 = 13$. Again we emphasize that this work is done in context, usually using a number line or other representation that helps students make sense of these algebraic strategies before symbolizing with variables.

Understanding each of these big ideas requires a shift in thinking beyond what students are used to in working with number. Students who do not construct these ideas will not be able to use algebraic expressions with meaning and will find manipulations involving equivalent expressions mysterious. The contexts in this unit enable students to construct these ideas by asking them to make sense of situations that require the ideas.

STRATEGIES

As you work with the activities in this unit, you will notice that students will use many strategies to derive answers. Here are some strategies to notice:

* ❖ **guessing and checking**

* ❖ **guessing, checking, and adjusting based on the result**

* ❖ **using equivalence to separate off equal amounts**

* ❖ **using equivalence or amounts of change to remove a variable**

* ❖ **symbolizing with variables**

* ❖ **justifying by doing several problems**

* ❖ **justifying by explaining why**

* ❖ **proving with all possible cases**

❖ Guessing and checking

Initially, when students are asked to determine the value of an unknown, they may guess and check using arithmetic procedures. They may just try different numbers until they find one that works. This strategy is an important arithmetic strategy in that it helps a student make sense of the situation and have expectations of an answer. However, a principal objective of this unit is to move students beyond guessing and checking so they construct pre-algebraic and algebraic strategies.

❖ Guessing, checking, and adjusting based on the result

As students reflect on the results and features of their trials, they begin to adjust accordingly. For example, if students are considering when 4 jumps and 8 steps is 52 steps and they try 10 steps per jump, they may notice that the result of 48 is four less than 52 and increase the jump by one step to find an answer. This refinement of the initial try, based on an understanding that the distance covered by four jumps increases as the steps in a jump increase, indicates a conceptual grasp of variation beyond what a second trial, of (for example) twelve, might indicate. Such strategies based on using and adapting the results of an initial trial are called pre-algebraic strategies because many students construct these strategies en route to developing more formal algebraic approaches.

❖ Using equivalence to separate off equal amounts

Recognizing and using equivalence explicitly is an algebraic approach that is developed throughout this unit. Students consider a context in which three jumps and six steps forward covers the same distance as four jumps forward and two steps backward. Since jumps are equal, students can (using the number line as a tool) *separate off* the fact that six steps forward is equivalent to one jump forward and two steps backward.

❖ Using equivalence or amounts of change to remove a variable

Later in the unit, students will consider a situation in which three jumps of Hopper equal four jumps of Skipper—a proportional situation. Situations like this require students to develop ways to separate off or remove multiples of these proportions. This use of equivalence, to rearrange another relationship rather than remove terms, is a sophisticated algebraic strategy.

❖ Symbolizing with variables

Finally, students begin to symbolize with variables, but great care is taken to ensure that the variables are used in a meaningful way. If three jumps and two steps are represented by $3j + 2s$, then the j needs to be interpreted as the length of a jump and not the noun *jump*. This usage is carefully developed through the use of context and the number line representation throughout the unit.

❖ Justifying by doing several problems

Initially, students think that proving means to try something out several times. When asked how they know it will always work, they justify by showing that it worked several times and they just keep showing that it works with more examples.

❖ Justifying by explaining why

One of the first major developments in students' thinking is realizing that just showing several examples is not a sufficient justification. They realize that they can never rule out the possibility that it won't work in some other example, and they can't try out infinite numbers of possibilities. At this point, students begin to recognize that a justification based on the reasoning behind the strategy may be more convincing and more generalizable.

❖ Proving with all possible cases

In this unit the combination chart is introduced as a way to generate all possible cases for using six-foot and eight-foot fence sections for a fence length of 66 feet. This tool provides students with a way to know with certainty and to formally prove (proof by all cases) that there are exactly three ways to build the fence of length 66: 11 sixes, 7 sixes and 3 eights, or 3 sixes and 6 eights.

MATHEMATICAL MODELING

Two models are developed in this unit—the double open number line and the combination chart. Unlike the number lines posted in many classrooms, an open number line does not contain the number sequence: instead, it indicates distances and "jumps" to illustrate the relationships between quantities. Only the numbers relevant to the situation are shown on the open number line. The open number line model supports students in visualizing relationships between numbers and unknown quantities as lengths. Since the open number line model is based on measurement, once students have constructed an understanding that numbers can represent length, they can represent relationships between numbers. Even unknown amounts, such as the length of a frog's jump, can be represented on the open number line, and the relationships between unknown lengths and known lengths can also be explored. The combination chart is a model that can be used to explore all possible cases and to examine patterns in exchanges.

Models go through three stages of development (Gravemeijer 1999; Fosnot and Dolk 2002):

❖ *model of the situation*

❖ *model of students' strategies*

❖ *model as a tool for thinking*

❖ Model of the situation

Initially, the models are introduced directly within the context. Arcs between points on a line represent both known and unknown lengths—the length of a bench length or fence section or the distance that a frog jumps. The combination chart is introduced in the context of needing a chart for customers who want to purchase varying quantities of six-foot and eight-foot fence sections.

❖ Model of students' strategies

Once models have been introduced to represent a situation, you can use them to model the students' strategies as they determine further relationships: if a student notices that four lengths of six is equivalent to three lengths of eight, then a sequence of four arcs representing six can be drawn on an open number line with the same start and end point as a sequence of three arcs of length eight. As you do the minilessons in this unit, you will be using the open number line to represent students' computation strategies for division and for solving for unknowns. The combination chart is used as a way to organize and record the exchanges and the addition of lengths.

❖ Model as a tool for thinking

Eventually students will be able to use the models as tools to think with—they will represent equivalent amounts on the number line and use them to transform relationships. The open number line is an important model to support the learning of the basic arithmetic operations with integers and fractions as well; it is used throughout other units in the *Contexts for Learning Mathematics* series. Many opportunities will arise to discuss the use of the open number line as you work through this unit. The combination chart becomes a helpful tool in producing all possible cases—a tool that can then be used to generate a formal proof.

A graphic with some components of the landscape of learning for the early development of algebra is provided on page 14. The purpose of the graphic is to allow you to see the longer journey of students' mathematical development and to place your work with this unit within the scope of this long-term development. You may also find it helpful to use this graphic as a way to record the progress of individual students for yourself. Each landmark can be shaded in as you find evidence in a student's work and in what the student says—evidence that a landmark strategy, big idea, or way of modeling has been constructed. In a sense, you will be recording the individual pathways students take as they develop as young mathematicians!

Research Connections

An excellent summary of research and issues in the teaching and learning of algebra can be found in the chapter, "Developing Mathematical Proficiency Beyond Number" in *Adding It Up: Helping Children Learn Mathematics* (National Research Council 2001).

A thorough research-based overview of many of the cognitive issues in the learning of algebra can be found in the chapter "The Learning and Teaching of School Algebra" in *The Handbook of Research on Mathematics Teaching and Learning* (Kieran 1992).

For a discussion of pre-algebraic strategies and the conceptual development of children's use of variables, we recommend the chapter, "Equations with Multiple Variables and Repeated Variables" in *Thinking Mathematically: Integrating Arithmetic & Algebra in Elementary School* (Carpenter, Franke, and Levi 2003). This book discusses the development of the concept of equality and relational thinking at grades earlier than those for which this unit is recommended.

For discussion of the use of the open number line as a representational tool in understanding number and operation, see *Young Mathematicians at Work: Constructing Fractions, Decimals, and Percents* (Fosnot and Dolk 2002) and *Young Mathematicians at Work: Constructing Number Sense, Addition, and Subtraction* (Fosnot and Dolk 2001).

References and Resources

Carpenter, Thomas P., Megan Loef Franke, and Linda Levi. 2003. *Thinking Mathematically: Integrating Arithmetic and Algebra in Elementary School.* Portsmouth, NH: Heinemann

Dolk, Maarten, and Catherine Twomey Fosnot. 2005a. *Fostering Children's Mathematical Development, Grades 5–8: The Landscape of Learning.* CD-ROM with accompanying facilitator's guide by Sherrin B. Hersch, Catherine Twomey Fosnot, and Antonia Cameron. Portsmouth, NH: Heinemann.

———. 2005b. *Minilessons for Operations with Fractions, Decimals, and Percents, Grades 5–8.* CD-ROMs with accompanying facilitator's guide by Antonia Cameron, Suzanne Werner, Catherine Twomey Fosnot, and Sherrin B. Hersch. Portsmouth, NH: Heinemann.

Fosnot, Catherine Twomey, and Maarten Dolk. 2001. *Young Mathematicians at Work: Constructing Number Sense, Addition, and Subtraction.* Portsmouth, NH: Heinemann.

———. 2002. *Young Mathematicians at Work: Constructing Fractions, Decimals and Percents.* Portsmouth, NH: Heinemann.

Fosnot, Catherine Twomey, and Bill Jacob. In preparation. Young Mathematicians at Work: The Role of Contexts and Models in the Emergence of Proof. In *Teachings and Learning Proof Across the Grades,* eds. D. Stylianous, M. Blanton, and E. Knuth. Mahwah, NJ: Lawrence Erlbaum Associates, Inc.

Gravemeijer, Koeno P.E. 1999. How emergent models may foster the constitution of formal mathematics. *Mathematical Thinking and Learning* 1 (2): 155–77.

Jeans, Sir James. Quoted in Newman, J.R., ed. 1956. *The World of Mathematics.* New York: Simon and Schuster.

Karlin, Samuel. 1983. Eleventh R. A. Fisher Memorial Lecture. Royal Society, April 20.

Kieran, Carolyn. 1992. The learning and teaching of school algebra. In *The Handbook of Research on Mathematics Teaching and Learning,* ed. Douglas Grouws. Reston, VA: National Council of Teachers of Mathematics.

Klein, Anton S., Meindert Beishuizen, and Adri Treffers. 2002. The empty number line in Dutch second grade. In *Lessons Learned from Research,* ed. Judith Sowder and Bonnie Schapelle. Reston, VA: National Council of Teachers of Mathematics.

National Research Council. 2001. *Adding It Up: Helping Children Learn Mathematics.* Washington, DC: National Academy Press.

Piaget, Jean. 1954. *The Construction of Reality in the Child.* London: Routledge and Kegan Paul.

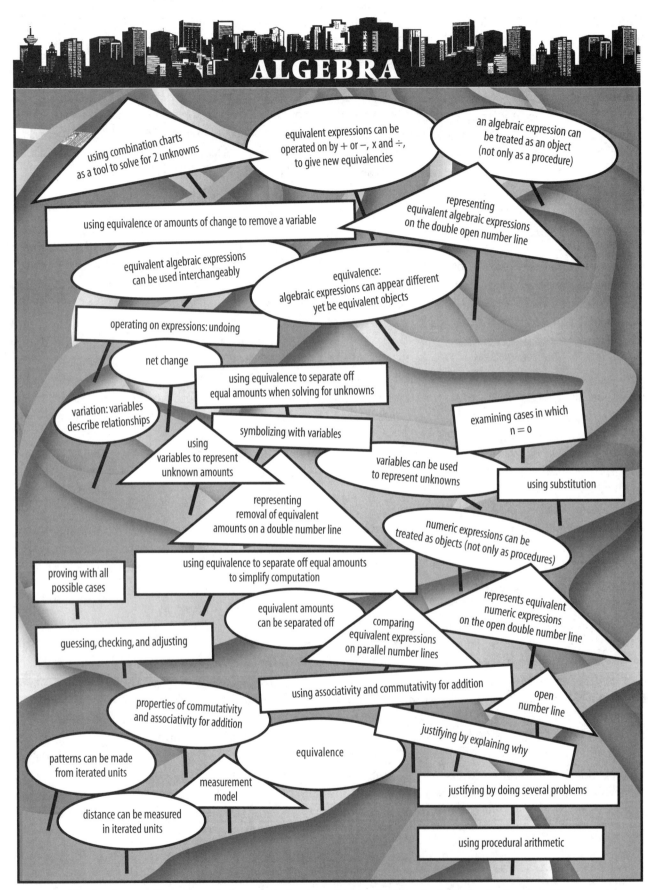

The landscape of learning: algebra on the horizon showing landmark strategies (rectangles), big ideas (ovals), and models (triangles).

Frog Jumping

Today you will develop the context of the California Frog-Jumping Contest—the context used throughout this unit. After listening to a description and a bit of the history of the Calaveras County contest, your students are introduced to a bullfrog, MT, and asked to investigate the length of his jump. The context of the frog-jumping contest is used to generate the open number line model—a model used throughout the unit to explore equivalence of algebraic expressions. As you move around the room supporting, encouraging, and conferring, you will notice various strategies as students solve for unknowns. These strategies and the open number line will become the focus of a subsequent math congress.

Day One Outline

Developing the Context

☀ Discuss the frog jump context and display the posters.

☀ Explain the referee's frog-jumping rule.

☀ Display an overhead transparency of Appendix C as you introduce the first investigation.

Supporting the Investigation

☀ Encourage students to consider drawing jumps on a number line to represent their thinking. This representation may help them see the relationship between the two jumping sequences.

Preparing for the Math Congress

☀ Ask students to make posters explaining the relationship between the two jumping sequences.

☀ Plan for a math congress that will highlight how students determined the equivalence by using a number line representation.

Facilitating the Math Congress

☀ Facilitate a discussion of the usefulness of the number line representation in determining the equivalence.

☀ Pose some additional frog jump questions designed to challenge students to generalize their findings.

Materials Needed

California frog-jumping contest poster

Frog on the jumping track poster

[If you do not have the full-color posters (available from Heinemann), you can use the smaller black-and-white versions in Appendixes A and B.]

Student recording sheet for the frog-jumping investigation (Appendix C)—one per pair of students

Before class, prepare an overhead transparency of Appendix C.

Overhead projector

Large chart paper— one sheet for each pair of students

Large chart pad and easel (or chalkboard or whiteboard)

Markers

Developing the Context

☀ Discuss the frog jump context and display the posters.

☀ Explain the referee's frog-jumping rule.

☀ Display an overhead transparency of Appendix C as you introduce the first investigation.

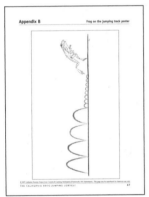

Convene your students in the meeting area. Display the poster of the California frog-jumping contest (or Appendix A) as you explain the following:

In California, in Calaveras County, a new sport was introduced more than 100 years ago: the frog jump. As many as 2,000 frogs compete each May at the Frogtown Fairgrounds in Calaveras County, Angel Camp, California. The world's frog jump record was set by Rosie the Ribbeter in 1986. She jumped 26 feet 5 ¾ inches!

"The contest was inspired by Mark Twain's 1865 fictional short story, The Celebrated Jumping Frog of Calaveras County. Over the years, the contest has become the most popular attraction at the Angel Camp annual fair, which also includes music, a craft show, and local talent. Today, some of the sidewalks of the city are lined with painted green frogs and bronze plaques, modeled on the Hollywood Walk of Fame." [Source: Faiza Elmasry. VOA News. January 9, 2003.]

Allow students to ask questions and discuss the contest to ensure that they can envision it. Suggest that they might want to find more information on the Internet and/or read Mark Twain's short story after math workshop. Then show the frog on the jumping track poster (or Appendix B) and continue:

Frogs spend most of their day sitting still. They catch flies or other insects with their tongues while they sit. Only occasionally do they jump, and that is usually to get to the water. So when they are placed on a jumping track, they usually sit and wait. When you command a frog "Jump!" usually it sits still and waits. To get frogs to jump, you usually need to encourage them with a slight touch on the back or maybe a few gentle touches before they get annoyed and decide to jump. When they do jump, they don't jump just once. Usually they take two, three, or more jumps and walk a little bit (a few steps in one direction or another).

So the behavior of frogs when they jump presents a special problem in competitions where you want to find out which frog has the biggest jump. This is because you have to figure out the length of a frog's jump when you know the length of several jumps and several steps combined. Referees of frog-jumping contests often use this rule:

The Referee's Frog-Jumping Rule: *Whenever a frog jumps in an event, if the frog takes more than one jump, all jumps are assumed to be equal in length and all steps are assumed to be equal in length.*

Invite the class to discuss why this rule would be used in frog-jumping contests. Various issues may come up—for example, the jumps might not really be equal or in a straight line. If students are concerned about this, you can explain that mathematicians often make certain assumptions that, although not perfect, make it possible to mathematize the problem. This is what the referee's frog-jumping rule does.

Now you can introduce MT and pose the first frog jump problems. Use the overhead transparency of Appendix C to introduce the first investigation. Assign math partners and provide each pair of students with a recording sheet (Appendix C).

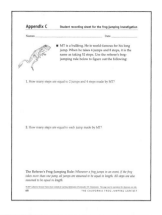

Supporting the Investigation

As students work, walk around and take note of the strategies and representations you see. Confer with pairs of students as needed to support and challenge. You will probably see the following strategies:

✦ Many students will use an "undoing" strategy. They will calculate the second problem first by subtracting 8 from 52 and then dividing by 4. This results in $j = 11$. Next they will use this result to answer the first question. As you confer, you might ask students if they think they could have answered the first question without knowing the answer to the second and how they might have done that. Encourage them to draw a representation of what the jumping sequences might look like on a number line and ask them to compare their sequences.

✦ Other students might begin by drawing what they know. You might encourage them to represent the jumps on a number line. A representation such as this may help students to realize that if $4j + 8 = 52$, then $2j + 4 = 26$, as it is half the distance. If they continue with this halving strategy, they will produce $j + 2 = 13$. At this point it is easy to see that a jump is equal to 11 steps.

☀ Encourage students to consider drawing jumps on a number line to represent their thinking. This representation may help them see the relationship between the two jumping sequences.

Conferring with Students at Work

Inside One Classroom

Sam: Alyssa and I don't know how to start.

Carlos (the teacher): Sometimes when mathematicians feel stuck, they try to draw a picture of what they know—they try to represent the situation with a mathematical model. Perhaps it would help to draw a number line and put the jumps and steps on it.

Author's Notes

Rather than telling Sam and Alyssa a way to begin, Carlos acknowledges that mathematicians often have the same problem. He suggests starting by trying to represent what they know.

continued on next page

continued from previous page

Sam: OK. Here's a picture of the first problem. But I don't know how big to make the jumps and I don't know where the steps end.
(Draws the following.)

Alyssa: I'll draw the original jumps.

Sam: It's just two of mine. See, it's 4 jumps and 8 steps.

Carlos: Hmmm…and that gets you to 52, right? I wonder…could you use this picture now to help you figure out what the size of the jump is?

Alyssa: Two jumps and 4 steps must be halfway…so half of 52… half of 50 is 25…26.

Carlos: Noticing that it was half really helped, didn't it. I wonder…could you keep doing that? Halving again?

Alyssa: Yeah. Maybe. So 1 jump and 2 steps is 13.

Sam: I'll draw that.

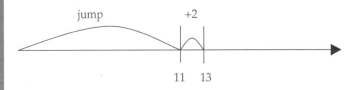

Hey! So the jump must be 11! Yeah, it's 11!

The representation helps the students realize the relationship between the two problems.

Carlos supports them in continuing to use the strategy, yet does so by wondering aloud. He offers an invitation, rather than a direction.

The students have not only solved the problem, they have learned that it sometimes helps to represent what you know as a way to start.

Preparing for the Math Congress

* Ask students to make posters explaining the relationship between the two jumping sequences.

* Plan for a math congress that will highlight how students determined the equivalence by using a number line representation.

After students have had a sufficient amount of time to work, ask them to prepare for a math congress on how the two questions are related and to represent this relationship on posters. As they prepare, make a note of which students have completed representations that will foster discussion of the big idea of equivalence. In this case, it is the equivalence of 4 jumps and 8 steps with two sets of 2 jumps and 4 steps.

▩ Tips for Structuring the Math Congress

Plan on choosing two pairs of students to share. Since the primary focus of the math congress is to develop a number line representation and to establish equivalence $4j + 8 = 2(2j + 4)$ look for students who have drawn representations of the problems, particularly students who can describe how the length of one expression is twice the length of the other. If several students have used an undoing strategy, you might want to discuss this briefly first and use a number line representation to match it, such as the following:

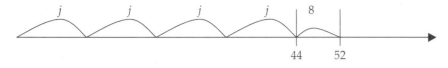

$4j + 8 = 52$

Students who have started with the second problem (like this) will probably now substitute 11 for the size of the jump to determine that $2j + 4 = 26$. This substitution may be the only way they see the relationship between the two problems. Once this strategy has been shared, ask if anyone thinks it is possible to answer the first question first. Start a discussion of equivalence by asking a group that can discuss the equivalence to share their work next.

Facilitating the Math Congress

Convene the students in the meeting area and have students share their posters. If no one has used a number line to represent the problems, ask students to draw the jumps and steps (or you can do it after their strategy is shared). Focus discussion on how the problems are related, asking students to consider the following:

☀ Facilitate a discussion of the usefulness of the number line representation in determining the equivalence.

☀ Pose some additional frog jump questions designed to challenge students to generalize their findings.

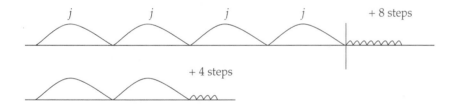

After the class is comfortable with the idea that two copies of the second diagram can be combined to make the first diagram, pose the following additional questions:

✦ What would happen if MT took one jump and two steps?

✦ How is this jump sequence related to the other jump sequences?

✦ What about three jumps and six steps?

✦ What other jumping sequences can we find values for without first finding the jump length?

Conclude the congress with a discussion about how the diagram is a useful representation for thinking about frog jump problems.

Behind the Numbers

This last set of questions has been crafted to challenge students to generalize. There are many other expressions that can be derived. For example, if $4j + 8 = 52$, then $8j + 16 = 104$, or if $j + 2 = 13$, then $3j + 6 = 39$ and $6j + 12 = 78$, etc. Students can also derive these equations in a variety of ways. For example, $3j + 6 = 39$ can be derived by multiplying both sides of the equation by 3. But students could also add or subtract—for example, $4j + 8 - (j + 2) = 52 - 13$.

Carlos (the teacher): So now that we've figured out how these problems are related, I'm wondering about a few more things. Could we use what we know to figure out 3 jumps and 6 steps? Talk with the person sitting next to you about this. *(After some pair talk, Carlos resumes whole-group conversation.)* Maria?

Maria: What Rosie and I think is that you can. It's 39...because a jump plus 2 steps is 13...so you can just three-times it.

(Carlos draws j + 2 three times and marks 13, 26, and 39 on the number line.)

Juan: Sam and I did it a different way. We subtracted a jump and 2 steps. That makes 3 jumps and 6 steps, too.

Carlos: Is this what you mean? *(Draws 4 jumps and 8 steps and then crosses out 1 jump and 2 steps.)* How do you know how many steps that is?

Juan: We subtracted. It's 52 − 13.

Carlos: Turn to the person next to you and talk about what Juan and Sam did. Why are they subtracting?

Alyssa: Oh, that's really cool. It works. And that means we could make lots and lots of ways. We can halve or double, and we can add or subtract.

Juan: Actually we can multiply or divide by any number...not just double or half.

Maria: Yeah. It's like if something is equal to something...then you can use those things and add 'em to other equal things...

Author's Notes

After establishing that the two problems are related and representing them on a number line model, Carlos begins to challenge the students to generalize.

Carlos uses pair talk to raise the key issue of the congress: expressions can be treated as objects that can be operated on.

Carlos uses the open number line to represent the relations.

Once again the relations are drawn on the open number line. Using the model in this way develops the use of the model as a tool to think with.

Students are beginning to generalize. Generalizing gets right to the heart of algebra.

Reflections on the Day

Today was devoted to developing representations. The context of frog jumps led to the use of the open number line and established the fact that algebraic expressions can be operated on to make other equivalent expressions, without always having to solve for the unknown. The work today developed the terrain for the journey ahead. As you continue with this unit, students will be encouraged and supported in substituting equivalent expressions as they solve for unknowns and work with simultaneous equations.

Jumping Buddies

The math workshop begins today with a division minilesson using a string of related problems. The division is represented on an open number line to help students explore the equivalent expressions. Then students work on more frog-jumping problems as a context for examining common multiples of 8 and 12. Equivalent expressions are represented on the open number line.

Day Two Outline

Minilesson: Keeping the Ratio Constant in Division

☀ Solicit a range of strategies as students solve a string of division problems. Record students' thinking on an open number line as a way to compare strategies and highlight the equivalent relationships among the problems.

Developing the Context

☀ Display an overhead transparency of Appendix D as you introduce the Frog and Toad investigation.

Supporting the Investigation

☀ Encourage students to draw number lines to represent their thinking.

☀ Once they have solved the problems, ask students to determine all the possible points where Frog's and Toad's jumps meet and to make posters of their findings.

Preparing for the Math Congress

☀ Conduct a "gallery walk" to give students a chance to review and comment on each other's posters.

☀ Plan for a congress discussion that will highlight the different ways of determining and representing equivalence.

Facilitating the Math Congress

☀ After all common landing points have been determined, focus the conversation on the distance between those points to highlight how common multiples and common factors are related.

Materials Needed

Student recording sheet for the Frog and Toad investigation (Appendix D)—one per pair of students

Before class, prepare an overhead transparency of Appendix D.

Overhead projector

Large chart paper—one sheet for each pair of students

Sticky notes—one pad per student

Large chart pad and easel

Markers

Minilesson: Keeping the Ratio Constant in Division
(10–15 minutes)

☀ Solicit a range of strategies as students solve a string of division problems. Record students' thinking on an open number line as a way to compare strategies and highlight the equivalent relationships among the problems.

This mental math minilesson uses a string of related problems to encourage students to examine division problems as expressions represented on an open number line. A double number line is a nice way to represent the relationships between these problems and will link the work on the string to the representation used throughout this unit. Write one problem at a time on chart paper and ask students to give a thumbs-up when they know the answer. When several thumbs are up, start discussion. Ask students to explain their reasoning, and represent the strategy on the open number line. Then ask for other strategies for the same question and have students compare them. After that, move to the next question. Invite students to discuss the connections between the problems and record these relationships. As you progress through the string, if you notice students beginning to discuss equivalence, invite a discussion on how such equivalence could help solve division problems.

Behind the Numbers

The first four problems are related. The first problem is likely to be an automatic fact for students, but by starting the string with it you can quickly represent six jumps of six landing at 36 on the number line. Students will probably realize that the answer to the second problem is double the answer to the first problem. Then you can write $2(36 \div 6) = 72 \div 6$ and represent the relationship on an open number line, as shown below:

If students do not immediately double, the partial quotients they use can also be represented on the double number line. For example, if a student uses the standard long division algorithm making use of $60 \div 6$ and $12 \div 6$, you can represent it as follows:

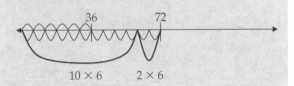

The third problem is equivalent to the first. Even if students do not initially realize or make use of the relationships, the relationships of the problems in the string and the representations on the double number line will support them in exploring these equivalencies. The figure below represents $72 \div 12 = 36 \div 6$

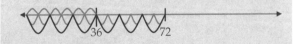

String of related problems:

$$36 \div 6 =$$
$$72 \div 6 =$$
$$72 \div 12 =$$
$$144 \div 24 =$$
$$42 \div 6 =$$
$$126 \div 18 =$$
$$425 \div 25 =$$

A Portion of the Minilesson

Author's Notes

Carlos (the teacher): OK. So the first one was easy. How about this one? Who has 72 ÷ 6? Show me with thumbs-up when you are ready. *(After most thumbs are up.)* Sharon?

Sharon: Twelve. The first one was 6 and this one is just double, because 72 is double 36.

Carlos: Let me represent what you said on the number line. *(Represents 6 jumps of 6 twice under the line. Six groups of 6 are on top of the line.)* And so can I write this? *(Writes:)*

By using the number line and writing the equation, Carlos provides his students with a visual representation of the equation.

$$2 (36 \div 6) = 72 \div 6$$

Turn to the person next to you and discuss this.

Pair talk is important here in order to ensure that everyone is involved in considering the equivalence.

Monique: It's like the frog jumps yesterday. Two of those fit into one.

Juan: Yeah.

Carlos: It's helpful to look at relationships in problems, isn't it? How about this one next? *(Writes:)*

$$72 \div 12$$

Monique: It's half of the last one.

Mathematicians look for and use equivalent relations. Carlos is encouraging his students to do the same.

Thomas: Yeah. It's the same as the first one, too. Six is twice 12—no, I mean if you double 6 you get 12 and if you double 36 you get 72. So it's the same. It's 6 again.

Carlos: So, Thomas, if I draw 6 sixes like this on the number line and then think of each jump as a 12, like this, then 6 twelves are double 36…

The representations drawn reflect students' thinking.

Thomas: Yeah. That's what I mean. Each 6 becomes a 12 down below. It's still 6 jumps. They're just twice as big.

Developing the Context

Math workshop continues with two more jumping problems. Use the overhead transparency of Appendix D to introduce students to Frog and Toad. Explain that when Frog jumps 8 times he lands on 96. Toad's jumps are equal to 8 of Frog's steps. Ask students to make drawings using open number lines as they did on Day One, to explore the Frog and Toad problems. Assign math partners and provide each pair with a recording sheet (Appendix D).

☀ Display an overhead transparency of Appendix D as you introduce the Frog and Toad investigation.

Behind the Numbers

Frog's jump problem is a partitive division question, meaning that it requires the distributing of the 96 steps into 8 equal jumps. The number of jumps is known but not the size (measured by number of steps in each jump). Students will need to determine that the size of Frog's jump is 12 steps. Toad's jump problem is a quotative division question. Here the size is known (8 steps) but the number of jumps (12) is not. Students need to determine how many groups of eight fit into 96. The relationship between partitive and quotative division is investigated in detail in *The Teachers' Lounge* (another unit in the *Contexts for Learning Mathematics* series), but is revisited here because it fosters conversation about the use of the number line representation for equivalent expressions. The question about where Frog and Toad meet involves finding common multiples of 8 and 12. The open number line facilitates this part of the inquiry.

☀ Encourage students to draw number lines to represent their thinking.

☀ Once they have solved the problems, ask students to determine all the possible points where Frog's and Toad's jumps meet and to make posters of their findings.

☀ Conduct a "gallery walk" to give students a chance to review and comment on each other's posters.

☀ Plan for a congress discussion that will highlight the different ways of determining and representing equivalence.

Supporting the Investigation

Some students may determine answers using previous knowledge about division. Encourage them to make a representation on an open number line anyway. As students delve into the mathematics of this unit, the representations they construct will be crucial for developing some of the big ideas about equivalence and algebra.

When students have determined the length of Frog's jump and the number of Toad's jumps, have them prepare posters that address the question: *At what points on the track do Frog and Toad both land?* Here are some of the strategies you might see:

✦ Marking off all 96 steps on the number line. Some students may have no other way to determine the mutual landing points except by marking every jump to determine the places where the jumps meet. As you confer, encourage these students to look at the patterns they are finding. Challenge them to anticipate the next mutual landing point without marking every step. Remind them that on an open number line not every number is indicated.

✦ Skip-counting by eight and by twelve and then circling the common multiples. As you confer, encourage these students to focus on the relationships between the two jumping sequences and illustrate these on two number lines, one directly above the other. This leads to a double number line representation. This way, the common multiples of 8 and 12 will become apparent as the locations where the jumps land in the same place.

✦ Using multiplication to derive common points, such as $3 \times 8 = 2 \times 12$, but not systematically finding all common multiples. As you confer, encourage these students to consider how they might know for certain that they have found all possible meeting points. This question may help them develop a way to produce all common multiples.

Preparing for the Math Congress

Explain that the class will have a gallery walk to look at the posters before convening for a math congress. Pass out small pads of sticky notes and suggest that everyone use them to make comments or to ask questions about each other's posters. These can be placed directly on the posters. Display all the posters around the room and have students spend about fifteen minutes walking around, reading and commenting on the mathematics on the posters. Give students a few minutes to read the comments and questions on their own posters and then convene a math congress.

You may need to model for your students how to comment in helpful and appropriate ways. You might write, "I think your strategy is interesting, and I'm trying to figure out why we have different answers." Or "You explained your work really well. I can understand what you did." Or "Your poster really convinces me. I agree with your thinking." Or "Your strategy is really great. What made you think of starting like that?" Or "Your way is so fast. I want to try that strategy next time!" Or "I'm puzzled about this step. I need more convincing."

■ Tips for Structuring the Math Congress

The purpose of this congress is to allow students to discuss their thinking about equivalence—for example, the fact that 6 toad jumps align with 4 frog jumps. Why is this? These are equivalent jumping sequences in terms of the distances covered. These equivalences should be visible on the number lines. Look for posters that represent this equivalence in different ways, such as $8 \times 6 = 12 \times 4$, or $8 + 8 + 8 + 8 + 8 + 8 = 12 + 12 + 12 + 12$, or skip-counting and circling common multiples. Discussion should center on the idea of the various equivalences given by common multiples. At the end, students should note that all the common multiples (24, 48, 72, 96) are multiples of the least common multiple, which is 24.

Facilitating the Math Congress

Ask students to join you in the meeting area. Have two or three pairs of students share the equivalent relationships they used in finding common landing points. After all common landing points have been found, ask students to consider the distance between the points. Ask students to reflect on why they are equally spaced.

☀ After all common landing points have been determined, focus the conversation on the distance between those points to highlight how common multiples and common factors are related.

Inside One Classroom

A Portion of the Math Congress

Carlos (the teacher): So let's see… It seems after looking at several strategies, we agree that 24, 48, 72, and 96 are the common points where Frog and Toad land. What is the distance between these points?

Juan: It's 24.

Carlos: Hmm…it's always 24. That's interesting. I wonder why it's always 24. Turn to the person next to you and discuss this.

Author's Notes

Now that students agree on the common points, Carlos challenges them to generalize.

Carlos models how mathematicians get intrigued with a pattern and wonder if, and why, it will continue.

continued on next page

continued from previous page

Nancy: *(After a few minutes of pair talk.)* Maybe it has something to do with…the meeting point has to be a number that can be divided by 8 and by 12. One times 8 and 1 times 12 don't work. Two times 8 doesn't work for 12, but 2 times 12 does work for 8.

Nancy proves her thinking by examining each case, starting with one-times, then two-times, etc.

Juan: I don't know what you mean.

Nancy: Well, 2 twelves are 24, and 8 goes into 24. So 24 works.

Juan: But why is it 24 every time?

Carlos: That's the question, isn't it?

Maria: Maybe because that's the smallest amount that works for both 8 and 12.

Nancy: Right. That's what I mean. One-times doesn't work, but two-times does. That's the smallest amount that works.

Juan: Oh…I get it: $2 \times 12 = 3 \times 8$. Look at the number line; each time they meet it starts over again. That's another $2 \times 12 = 3 \times 8$ and that's why it's 24 each time. It just happens again on the number line…

Maria: Six times 4 equals 24 too.

Carlos: Say more about that, Maria.

Maria has made an interesting mathematical observation here and Carlos maximizes the moment by asking her to say more.

Maria: Well, I don't know if it matters, but I was just thinking…we said the number had to be a number that 8 and 12 went into, right? Eight is 2 fours, and 12 is 3 fours.

Juan: Yeah…so?

Maria: So 2×3 is 6 and 6 fours is 24. So maybe that 6 is the number of fours needed.

Maria is examining the relationships differently by factoring.

Carlos: How many people can put in their own words what Maria is saying?

By asking for paraphrasing, Carlos is able to determine how many students are following Maria's thinking. The class is now discussing a big idea: how are common multiples and common factors related?

Reflections on the Day

The work today focused on equivalent expressions and their representation on the number line. In the minilesson, students explored division. The investigation of Frog's and Toad's jumps provided a context for students to think about common multiples and equivalent expressions. The number line used to represent unknown jump lengths became a tool for considering the relationships among different common multiples.

DAY THREE
The Benches

Today students consider a new context of placing benches alongside two frog-jumping tracks. The benches come in six-foot and eight-foot lengths and the tracks are 28 feet and 42 feet long. Students work with partners investigating how many benches of each size are needed for the tracks. They make posters of the important ideas they want to share in a math congress, to be held on Day Four.

Day Three Outline

Developing the Context

☀ Introduce and discuss the bench investigation, highlighting the requirement that the bench lengths must add up to the length of the track.

Supporting the Investigation

☀ Prompt students to find all possible solutions and encourage them to think about the relationships between the solutions.

☀ Introduce an additional constraint to the problem that requires students to use a combination of both bench sizes for one side of the track.

Preparing for the Math Congress

☀ Pose two new questions and ask students to make posters that include justifications for their answers.

☀ Plan for a congress discussion on equivalence and how equivalence can be represented using a double number line.

Facilitating the Math Congress

☀ Highlight the ideas of equivalence and exchange by focusing the congress discussion on how students know they have found all the possible bench combinations.

Materials Needed

Student recording sheets for the bench investigation (Appendix E)—one per pair of students

Length 6 and 8 Cuisenaire rods or connecting cubes, as needed

Drawing paper— a few sheets per pair of students

Large chart paper— one sheet for each pair of students

Large chart pad and easel

Markers

Developing the Context

☀ Introduce and discuss the bench investigation, highlighting the requirement that the bench lengths must add up to the length of the track.

On chart paper, draw the following diagram as you introduce today's investigation:

28-foot jumping track

42-foot jumping track

Behind the Numbers

The numbers in this scenario have been chosen deliberately. There is a unique way to build each of the 28-foot lengths (2 six-foot and 2 eight-foot benches can be put together for each side of the track). However, there are two possible ways to build each of the 42-foot lengths, either with 7 six-foot benches, or with 3 six-foot benches and 3 eight-foot benches.

Most students will find through trial and error a combination of benches that can be used to line the tracks. However, the important mathematics for this unit arises when students are pushed to think about finding other possibilities and to verify that they have found them all. The big idea of equivalence emerges when students are able to see that 4 six-foot benches cover the same distance as 3 eight-foot benches. This leads to an important algebraic strategy (substitution) because 7 six-foot benches on one side can be replaced by 3 six-foot benches and 3 eight-foot benches. It is therefore critical to push all students to consider the second question about the possibility of more than one combination.

The context of placing benches on both sides of the track has also been chosen intentionally. Many students will draw a rectangle and mark off six-foot lengths and eight-foot lengths on opposite sides of their drawings to represent the sections they are using, or they will see the benches as two parallel lines. Representations of this type will be used as a problem-solving tool throughout this unit when students work on a variety of algebraic questions using a double number line. It is important that students include their representations on the posters they will make later today. Those students who have constructed the equivalence of 4 six-foot benches with 3 eight-foot benches should be able to show this equivalence on their representations.

The frogs are planning a jumping contest. They have two jumping tracks; one is 28 feet long and the other is 42 feet long. They have decided to bring in benches from their storeroom and place them along both sides of each track end to end so the benches line the track lengths exactly. The benches in the storeroom are of two different lengths. One size is six feet long and the other size is eight feet long. How many six-foot benches should they get and how many eight-foot benches should they get in order to line both sides of both tracks? Help them make a list.

Facilitate an initial discussion in the meeting area before the students set to work. Discuss the requirement that the bench lengths add up to the length of the track. Make sure students realize that no bench can be cut. Allow students to put forth their initial thoughts and then suggest that they work in pairs to answer two questions:

✦ How many six-foot benches and how many eight-foot benches are needed in order to line both tracks?

✦ Are there other possible choices of six- and eight-foot benches that could be used?

Assign math partners and give each pair of students a recording sheet (Appendix E). Ask students to work only on the first two problems in Appendix E. Make bins of Cuisenaire rods or connecting cubes available for students to use if they wish.

Supporting the Investigation

As students work, walk around and take note of the strategies you see. Confer with pairs of students as needed to support and challenge them in their investigations.

☀ Prompt students to find all possible solutions and encourage them to think about the relationships between the solutions.

☀ Introduce an additional constraint to the problem that requires students to use a combination of both bench sizes for one side of the track.

Inside One Classroom

Conferring with Students at Work

Thomas: We can't make a length 28 using just 8-foot or just 6-foot benches because 6 and 8 don't go into 28.

Alyssa: But we can mix them up. What if we use 3 sixes?

Thomas: OK, that's 6, 12, 18. *(Draws each jump of 6 on the drawing of a bench.)* But that leaves 10 more. That can't work either. Can we cut a bench?

Carlos (the teacher)**:** No, we can't cut the benches. Alyssa said you can mix them up. Are there other ways to do that?

Alyssa: If we do 2 sixes, that's 12, which leaves…16. That's 2 eights. Hey, 2 sixes and 2 eights work!

John: *(Working with Meg on the 42-foot track.)* If we have 4 eights, that's 32, and if we have 2 sixes, it's 12, so together that is, um, 44. It's too much.

Meg: But it's only 2 too much, so let's switch an 8 and a 6.

John: Yeah, that cuts it back to 42 and we have 3 eights and 3 sixes.

Author's Notes

At first Carlos just listens as students work. It is often best to do this in order to understand students' ideas and strategies. Students' initial ideas are always the beginning place of a good conference.

Many students will draw each attempt on the picture of the track. This is important because this type of representation will become a tool for the work to come.

Carlos helps to define the problem. The benches cannot be cut.

Although guess and check is common initially, trial and adjustment is an important advance in strategy. This type of thinking, which can be illustrated on the representation (as the decomposition 8 = 6 + 2), is a precursor to the formal algebraic operations students will learn later.

Many students who find a single solution may think they have completed the task so it is important to ask, "Are there other ways to put benches together?" As students try to find all possible solutions, here are a few strategies that you might see:

✦ adding up sixes and eights to see what they add up to
[See Figure 1, page 30]

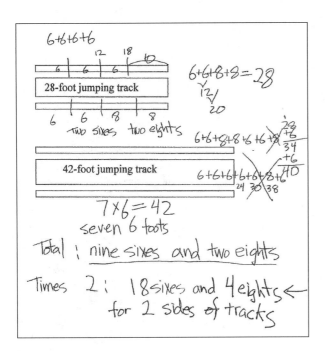

Figure 1

Behind the Numbers

These constraints are chosen so that students will have to use both combinations for one side of the 42-foot track. If they used only six-foot pieces for the 42-foot length, they would need 18 six-foot sections in total, and if they used 3 eight-foot sections on each of the 42-foot lengths, they would need 10 eight-foot sections in total. In making a diagram to represent the solution with different bench combinations for the 42-foot track, the students will in essence be constructing a *double number line* in which the two solutions are represented above and below each other on parallel lines. Within this representation the equivalence of 3 eight-foot sections with 4 six-foot sections is also apparent.

Figure 2

◆ making a list of all the multiples of 6 and a list of all the multiples of 8 and then adding various combinations of these multiples together to see which add to 28 and 42 *[See Figure 2]*

Both of these strategies are *arithmetical;* they are based upon knowledge of computation. Since a primary goal of this unit is for students to construct *algebraic* strategies, it is important to push students to think about the relationships between the solutions. Note students who begin to exchange and substitute equivalent bench combinations. For example, 4 six-foot benches can be exchanged for 3 eight-foot benches. The exchanging of equivalent pieces is a more algebraic strategy.

Once several groups have found both solutions to length 42, the following question should be posed to the class:

While you are working, let me tell you one more part of the story. When the frogs went to the storeroom, they found that they had only 17 six-foot benches and 9 eight-foot benches. Will these amounts work? What should they do?

Ask students to investigate the third problem in Appendix E.

Preparing for the Math Congress

After students have had a sufficient amount of time and are familiar with the context and the possible combinations of benches, ask them to prepare for a math congress by making posters. The posters should address the following two questions, which are more explicit than the original questions that the class has been investigating:

✦ *The frogs decide they want new benches so they go out to price benches at different stores. What are their options for buying six-foot and eight-foot benches to place along both sides of both their 28- and 42-foot tracks?*

✦ *Explain how you know you have found all the possibilities.*

Have a short discussion with the class about the nature of these new questions. Students are being asked not only to list answers, but to explain how they know they have all the possibilities. Explain that what they write on their posters needs to be clear for others to understand. The posters should not be just a copy of the students' draft notes. The posters should present concise, clear arguments or justifications for how the students know they have found all the options.

Mathematicians write up their mathematics for math journals. In these articles, they do not merely reiterate everything they did. Instead, they craft a proof or argument for other mathematicians. Doing this not only generates further reflection, it focuses the author on developing a convincing and elegant argument—an important part of mathematics. Of course, elementary students are not expected to write formal proofs, but by focusing on the justification and logic of their arguments you are helping them develop the ability to write their ideas for presentation in a mathematical community. For example, if students have constructed the idea that an exchange of 4 six-foot sections with 3 eight-foot sections doesn't change the length, they should be able to explain why there is only one solution for the 28-foot track—no exchanges are possible.

▨ Tips for Structuring the Math Congress

Examine the posters as students are preparing them and think about how you want the math congress conversation to flow. Plan on structuring the congress to discuss the big ideas related to equivalence and also to show how these ideas can be represented with double number lines. Noting the students' struggles and strategies will help you decide which students you will ask to share and the issues you will raise for discussion.

☀ Pose two new questions and ask students to make posters that include justifications for their answers.

☀ Plan for a congress discussion on equivalence and how equivalence can be represented using a double number line.

Facilitating the Math Congress

☀ Highlight the ideas of equivalence and exchange by focusing the congress discussion on how students know they have found all the possible bench combinations.

Convene the students in the meeting area to discuss a few of the ideas on the posters. Rather than having students just share the strategies they used, focus conversation on the second question: how they know that the three possibilities are all the possibilities that can be found. Have students address the big idea of equivalence and exchange. Look for opportunities to connect this idea with the work on other posters where it may not be expressed as clearly.

A Portion of the Math Congress

Inside One Classroom

Carlos (the teacher): Let's start with you, José and Lupe. You noticed something about replacing eights by sixes. Tell us about it.

Lupé: For the small track, the 28, we knew that 2 sixes and 2 eights worked. If you try to replace any eight by a six it gets 2 smaller, and if you do it twice it gets 4 smaller and then you are stuck. So there aren't any more ways to do it.

José: But with the bigger track we knew that 3 sixes and 3 eights worked and if you take 3 eights out and put in 3 sixes then you are 6 too small. You can fix that by putting in another six. So 7 sixes works.

Lupé : And 6 times 7 is 42 so that also shows why it works.

Carlos: How does that show we know we have all the solutions?

Lupé: Because we can't go any smaller or bigger.

Carlos: Can someone put what Lupe is saying in your own words? Tara?

Tara: Well, 3 sixes and 3 eights work for the long track. If we want to do it a different way, say more sixes, we put a six in and take an eight out, but then it is 2 shorter. So we do that 3 times and then have 6, I mean 7, sixes. But you can't take any more eights out so that's all of them. That's why you did them all.

Alfonso: But what about if you want less sixes?

Tara: But if you take sixes out and put eights in, it gets bigger.

Alfonso: If you take a six out and don't put an eight in, it gets smaller.

Tara: Yeah, but then it gets too small because there are only 3 sixes and you can't put eights back in to fix it.

Author's Notes

Carlos starts by asking two students to share a general observation they have made. This move implicitly suggests that part of doing mathematics is communicating and justifying thinking to a community of other mathematicians.

Discussion is welcomed and flows naturally in a congress.

Here Carlos directs the conversation toward the central issue of justifying the claim that all the possibilities have been found.

Asking for clarification and paraphrasing ensures that students understand each other's ideas and can discuss them.

Students defend their thinking—the teacher doesn't do it for them.

continued on next page

continued from previous page

Alfonso: I get it. You would have to take 4 sixes out and put 3 eights back in to make it the same. So there can't be any more than the two ways we have.

Carlos: Who else noticed something about the 4 sixes and the 3 eights? Maria?

Carlos pushes the community to carefully consider the equivalence of 4 x 6 and 3 x 8.

Maria: They're the same. They both are 24.

Carlos: Tell us more. Explain how that helps.

Maria: It's like what Alfonso said. If you take out 4 sixes and put in 3 eights, it doesn't change anything.

Alyssa: It's because 24 is a common multiple of 6 and 8. So you can make a switch and get new combinations. But you can't make any smaller switches. That's why we get all of them.

Carlos: I think Maria and Alyssa have a big idea here. I want you to take a minute here and talk with your partner about how this number 24 helps us find the possibilities.

Pair talk is used to engage all the students in considering equivalence.

▦ Assessment Tips

The posters are probably too large to place in students' portfolios. If this is the case, you can take a photograph of each of them and staple the photograph to a blank page for your anecdotal notes. Make notes about the strategies and big ideas described in the unit overview (pages 8–11). Do you have evidence that any of these ideas and strategies have been constructed?

Reflections on the Day

Several big ideas about equivalence were explored today as students investigated the benches. Some groups probably used trial and error to find the possibilities while other groups may have adjusted their initial trials to find solutions. By using organized lists or by making exchanges, students were able to find the different possible solutions to the problem. The context of the problem enabled students who started with arithmetical strategies to use more algebraic approaches. The algebraic approaches, using equivalence and substitution, enabled students to show why their collection of possibilities was complete as they worked to develop proofs.

The Fence

Materials Needed

Students' posters from Day Three

Student recording sheet for the fence investigation (Appendix F)—one per pair of students

Before class, prepare an overhead transparency of Appendix F.

Overhead projector

Large chart paper—one sheet per pair of students

Large chart pad and easel

Markers

Math workshop begins today with a minilesson using a double number line to represent distance that can be traveled using various amounts of gas. Students then have an opportunity to apply the ideas of equivalence developed on Day Three to a problem about building fences around the frog-jumping arena.

Day Four Outline

Minilesson: A String of Related Problems

☀ Work on a string of problems designed to highlight proportional reasoning.

☀ Use a double number line representation to highlight a range of student strategies.

Developing the Context

☀ Display a transparency of Appendix F as you explain the parameters of the fence investigation.

Supporting the Investigation

☀ As students work, encourage them to find ways to keep track of the possibilities they generate and to consider the relationships among those possibilities.

☀ If students are still using arithmetical strategies, encourage them to consider the equivalence and substitution strategies developed on Day Three.

Minilesson: A String of Related Problems (10–15 minutes)

This mental math minilesson uses a string of related problems that encourages students to examine proportional relationships on a double number line. Do one question at a time, collecting multiple strategies and representing them on a double number line with the number of miles on top and number of gallons on the bottom. For example, if students say five gallons is a third of the way, so that is ⅓ of 360, you would draw the following:

- ☀ Work on a string of problems designed to highlight proportional reasoning.

- ☀ Use a double number line representation to highlight a range of student strategies.

String of related problems:

Mr. Garcia can drive 360 miles on a full tank of 15 gallons of gas.

How far can Mr. Garcia drive on 5 gallons?

How far can Mr. Garcia drive on 3 gallons?

How about 8 gallons?

How about 4 gallons?

How about 1 gallon?

How many gallons would Mr. Garcia need to drive 600 miles?

Behind the Numbers

The first problem makes use of the landmark number of five. Also, 360 is a number for which it is fairly easy to take ⅓. These three portions (the 120 for each of the thirds) can then be marked on the double number line. The second problem brings up the relationship of multiplication and division: ⅓ of 15 = 5; ⅕ of 15 = 3. The third problem can be solved by adding the results of the first two problems. The next problem is half of that result. As the string continues, students will most likely begin to use a variety of relationships. Add more numbers to the string if you like.

Developing the Context

Display a transparency of Appendix F as you tell the following story:

> *The frogs want to build a fence to enclose a rectangular area to be their jumping arena. The arena is 52 feet by 66 feet. They can buy fencing in six-foot and eight-foot lengths. What are all the possible choices of six-foot and eight-foot sections of fencing to go all around the arena? They do not want to cut these fence sections and they cannot bend them around a corner. One six-foot section will come with a gate. Help the frogs prepare a shopping list for the different possibilities so they can buy enough sections of fence.*

Assign math partners and give each pair of students a recording sheet (Appendix F).

- ☀ Display a transparency of Appendix F as you explain the parameters of the fence investigation.

Behind the Numbers

This problem is the same type as the one investigated on Day Three. However, because of the greater numbers, students are pushed to go beyond the guess-and-check strategy and use the equivalence and substitution strategies they developed. Because there are more possibilities this time, students are also challenged to organize their work and record possible exchanges. Again, the numbers in this scenario have been chosen purposefully. Each length is 24 more than in the previous scenario, so students could obtain initial solutions by adding 4 sixes or 3 eights to the solutions for the benches. However, it is more likely that students will start over, finding an initial combination and modifying it by using equivalent exchanges to find the other possibilities.

The numbers have also been chosen because they can lead to a variety of recording strategies when trying to determine the combinations. When the multiples of 6 and 8 are aligned on a double number line (groups of sixes marked on one line, groups of eights marked on a parallel one just below), the common multiples of 6 and 8 are apparent as meeting points. This representation was discussed on Day Three and students can revisit it today.

☀ As students work, encourage them to find ways to keep track of the possibilities they generate and to consider the relationships among those possibilities.

☀ If students are still using arithmetical strategies, encourage them to consider the equivalence and substitution strategies developed on Day Three.

Supporting the Investigation

Since students have had experience with this type of problem, they will probably have strategies to get started. (It may be helpful to provide students with their posters from Day Three.) However, because of the larger numbers they will need to organize their work more carefully to keep track of all the possibilities they will generate. As you confer, encourage students to find ways to organize and keep track of the possibilities they find.

As you move around the room, take note of the various strategies you see. If students are using only the arithmetical strategy of guess and check, encourage them to think about some of the ideas discussed in the earlier congress to see if they could use these ideas to save time. Here are a few of the strategies you may see:

✦ a sequence of diagrams with possibilities determined by arithmetic [See Figure 3, page 37]

✦ number lines for each of 52 and 66, with solutions shown and the substitutions of 4 sixes for 3 eights as double number lines [See Figure 4, page 37]

✦ listing all the multiples of 6 and all the multiples of 8 and then adding various combinations of these multiples together to see which add to 52 [See Figure 5, page 37]

✦ a chart showing one possibility (such as 6 six-foot pieces and 25 eight-foot pieces) and then the corresponding numbers that arise by making successive exchanges [See Figures 6 and 7, page 37]

If students have found several possibilities for choosing six- and eight-foot sections, have them think about the relationships among these possibilities. If ready, they can begin to make posters describing the possibilities they found and the relationships among them. They will finish their posters on Day Five and have a congress about the possibilities then.

■ Assessment Tips

As you move around and confer, note whether students seem to realize that all the possibilities can be obtained from a single possibility through repeated exchanges. Which students continue to guess and check? Which students make an organized list to determine the solutions? How do the students represent their strategies? Is the number line a useful tool for their thinking, or do they use their number sense instead?

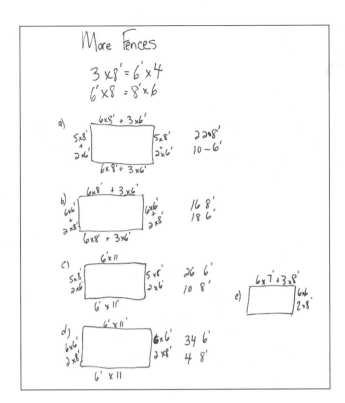

Figure 3

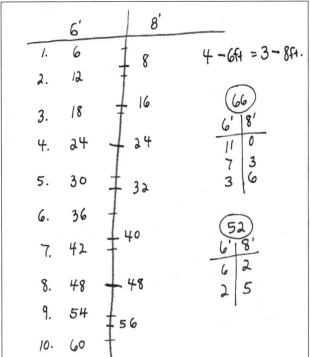

Figure 6

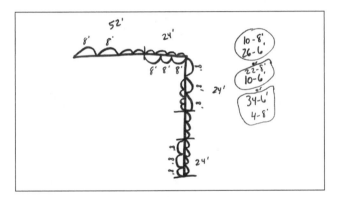

Figure 4

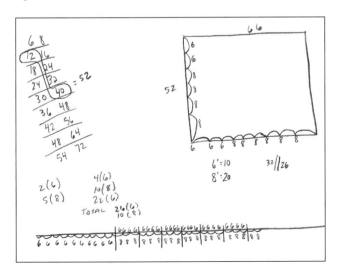

Figure 5

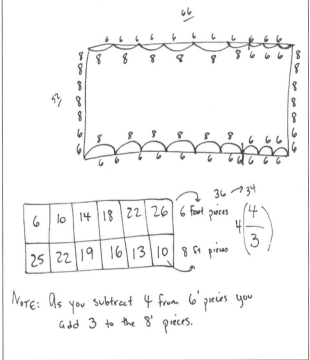

Figure 7

Differentiating Instruction

As you move around the room, differentiate by supporting and helping students in developmentally appropriate ways. Note the different strategies they are using. Stay grounded in the context to help students realize the meaning of what they are doing; refer to fences and diagrams rather than discussing the numbers involved abstractly. Encourage the students to think about what would happen if they removed eight-foot sections and replaced them by six-foot sections. Have them draw lines on the recording sheets to illustrate the different possibilities and the relationships among the possibilities.

Reflections on the Day

Today began with a minilesson on how far Mr. Garcia could travel if he can drive 360 miles with 15 gallons of gas. The proportional reasoning students used was recorded on a double number line. Then students discussed strategies for building various lengths of fencing out of six-foot and eight-foot sections, exploring the use of common multiples and the substituting of equivalent expressions. They used these ideas to tackle more complex problems and were challenged to keep track, and to represent these algebraic exchanges by using a double number line.

The Combination Chart and Exchanges

Today the students hold a congress based on the fence problem that they investigated on Day Four. During the congress you will facilitate construction of a combination chart to represent the different combinations of six- and eight-foot fence sections. The big ideas of equivalence and the results of exchanging sixes for eights from the previous days are explored on this chart.

Day Five Outline

Preparing for the Math Congress

☀ Have students prepare posters detailing the possible combinations of fence sections they explored on Day Four. Explain that the posters should also address the relationships between the possibilities and how students know they have found them all.

☀ Conduct a gallery walk to give students a chance to review and comment on each other's posters.

☀ Ask students to discuss with their partners how they might make a chart to keep track of the different ways to combine fence sections.

Facilitating the Math Congress

☀ Discuss students' suggestions for how to compile a chart of fence section combinations.

☀ Display a transparency of Appendix G and discuss strategies for filling out the chart as a way to highlight the exchange of equivalent amounts.

☀ Distribute copies of Appendix G and ask students to complete the charts and consider several questions about the relationships among the numbers in the chart.

☀ Reconvene a whole-class meeting to discuss the connections between the solutions on the students' posters and the patterns in the numbers on their charts.

Materials Needed

Students' posters from Day Four

Combination chart (Appendix G)—one per pair of students

Before class, prepare an overhead transparency of Appendix G.

Overhead projector and marker

Sticky notes—one pad per student

Preparing for the Math Congress

☀ Have students prepare posters detailing the possible combinations of fence sections they explored on Day Four. Explain that the posters should also address the relationships between the possibilities and how students know they have found them all.

☀ Conduct a gallery walk to give students a chance to review and comment on each other's posters.

☀ Ask students to discuss with their partners how they might make a chart to keep track of the different ways to combine fence sections.

Have the students continue their work from Day Four by preparing (or finishing) posters showing the different possible combinations of six-foot and eight-foot sections they could use for building a fence around the jumping arena. Students should illustrate the relationships between the possibilities and describe how they know they have all of them. Then explain that the class will have a gallery walk to look at the posters before you start a congress. Pass out small pads of sticky notes and suggest that everyone use them to make comments or to ask questions. These can be placed directly on the posters. Display all the posters around the room and allow about ten minutes for everyone to walk around, reading and commenting on the mathematics on the posters. Give the students a few additional minutes to read the comments and questions on their own posters and then ask everyone to consider the following question:

> *Suppose we wanted to make a chart that would help fence designers understand their options for building different fences. How might we do that? How could the strategies from yesterday help us? Take a look at the posters and think about the various strategies we developed.*

Have students discuss this question with their partners for a few minutes and circulate around the room making notes of the strategies students are discussing. Then pull the class together for a congress.

Often mathematicians solve problems by stepping back and considering a more general question than originally posed. This provides an opportunity to think more deeply about *relationships* instead of the specific procedures to get the answer in the original case. This process of generalizing, which will be modeled in today's congress, is an important part of learning algebra. Instead of going through the various approaches to build fences of lengths 52 and 66, the class will construct a combination chart, which will, among other things, include different ways to combine six-foot and eight-foot lengths to make a total of 52 or 66 feet. However, its organization is what is of special interest here. Every "move" from one entry of the chart to another corresponds to adding or subtracting lengths. In this way, all of the exchanges considered on previous days can be represented on the chart.

Facilitating the Math Congress

☀ Discuss students' suggestions for how to compile a chart of fence section combinations.

☀ Display a transparency of Appendix G and discuss strategies for filling out the chart as a way to highlight the exchange of equivalent amounts.

☀ Distribute copies of Appendix G and ask students to complete the charts and consider several questions about the relationships among the numbers in the chart.

Open the congress by explaining to the class that since the posters were examined during the gallery walk, there is no need to share solutions and methods for solving the fence problem during the congress. Instead, the congress will consider the more general problem of making a chart to help people build fences of different lengths. The approach taken in the congress may depend upon the approaches students have come up with to make the chart. Here is one possible way to structure the congress.

Open the discussion by considering the cases in which there is only one type of fence section. Have students share what the possibilities are in these cases. Then display this information in a combination chart using the transparency of Appendix G. Have the class discuss strategies for filling out the chart.

☀ Reconvene a whole-class meeting to discuss the connections between the solutions on the students' posters and the patterns in the numbers on their charts.

A Portion of the Math Congress

Inside One Classroom

Author's Notes

Carlos (the teacher): So let's make a chart that can help anybody make a shopping list for a fence. Clarissa, you were talking about what if there were no 8-foot sections. Then there would be some problems for fence makers. Tell us about that.

Carlos begins by posing the problem generated by one of the students: What if there were no eight-foot sections? Now there is a reason to have a chart.

Clarissa: Juan and I were saying that if the store ran out of 8-foot sections, it would be bad because you could only do multiples of 6, like 6, 12, and 18 and so on.

Carlos: Well, that might happen. And what if you wanted to build a 30-foot fence?

Juan: That would be OK because you are lucky. You could use 6-foot sections. You'd need 5 of them.

Carlos: So let's start our chart by putting that information down.
(Begins to develop the combination chart with Clarissa's observation.)

6	12	18	24	30	36	42	48
1	2	3	4	5	6	7	8

Number of 6-foot sections

Does this look OK, Clarissa and Juan?

Juan: Yeah, that's it.

Carlos: But what if we had the opposite problem? Say the store only had 8-foot sections?

Carlos models the importance of looking at both extremes.

Alyssa: Then we'd have to write out the eights. Like 16, 24, and so on.

Carlos: OK. But what I'm going to do is write them as a column instead of a row. Like this:

continued on next page

continued from previous page

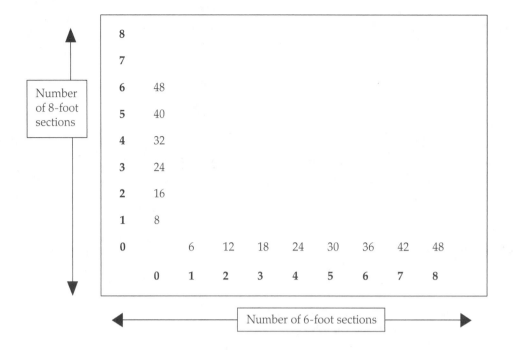

Number of 8-foot sections

Number of 6-foot sections

Carlos: Any thoughts on why I'm doing it this way? Why rows and columns? Talk to your partner for a minute and see if you can find out why. *(After a few minutes of pair talk.)* Rosie, what's your theory?

Rosie: I think you made a big rectangle with rows and columns so you can put in all the other numbers.

Sam: I don't get it. What other numbers?

Rosie: So we can combine them. Look. If you have 1 six and 1 eight, that's 14 and you can put it here. *(Points to cell above the 6 and to the right of 8).*

Sam: Oh. You mean we should just add them up and fill them in? Like adding 12 and 8 and putting in 20 in the next spot.

Carlos: We could. Would a chart like this be helpful?

Sam: I guess. Customers could just read off the chart then.

(Class works to add numbers and Carlos inserts them in the appropriate cells.)

Ramiro: We could just go across and add 6 each time. That might be easier.

Carlos: Explain what you mean.

Ramiro: Next to the 34. It would be 40, then 46.

Carlos continues building the combination chart first with the extremes. Then he encourages the students to examine the layout of the chart. Is this organization helpful? Why? What might go next?

continued on next page

continued from previous page

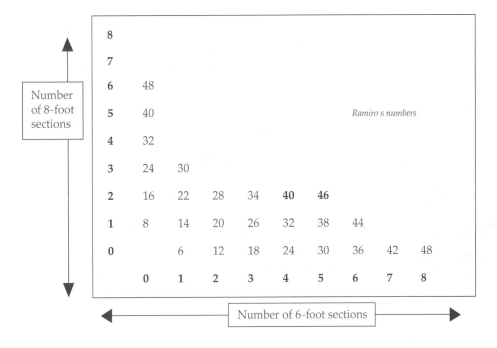

The chart shows "Number of 8-foot sections" on the vertical axis and "Number of 6-foot sections" on the horizontal axis, labeled "Ramiro's numbers."

	0	1	2	3	4	5	6	7	8
8									
7									
6	48								
5	40								
4	32								
3	24	30							
2	16	22	28	34	**40**	**46**			
1	8	14	20	26	32	38	44		
0		6	12	18	24	30	36	42	48

Carlos: Why does this work? Why does Ramiro's strategy work?

Charlene: I think it is because each time you are adding another 6-footer. Yeah, that's it. Each time there is one more 6-foot piece so the fence grows by 6.

Carlos adds Ramiro's numbers, but asks the community to consider if his strategy works.

After a few strategies have been discussed and students seem able to continue filling in the chart on their own, distribute one copy of the chart (Appendix G) to each pair of students. Ask them to complete the chart and then to consider the following questions:

+ *What happens when you go up two rows? Why do the numbers on the chart go up by 16?*

+ *What happens when you go up one row and then to the left one column?*

+ *What happens if you go down two rows and over three columns? Why?*

+ *The number 30 is on the chart twice. What does that mean? Why did that happen? What kind of exchange is happening?*

+ *Where do 52 and 66 appear? Why there? Are those solutions on the posters?*

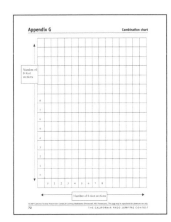

It is important to link the information in the students' charts to their posters. So after allowing students a sufficient amount of time to work on their charts, invite the students back to the meeting area for further whole-group discussion of the questions. Make sure that students understand what the numbers on the chart represent. Have several students explain where their work on the posters can be located on the combination chart. Wonder aloud why all the solutions on the posters can be found along the same line: each is down three and over four from the one before it. Discussion of the reason brings the congress full circle to the big idea of equivalence: this relationship on the chart is another way to represent the equivalence of 3 eights and 4 sixes. Since all the possible combinations are listed, students can be sure that there are exactly three ways to build a fence of length 66: 11 sixes, 7 sixes and 3 eights, or 3 sixes and 6 eights.

Reflections on the Day

Students completed their work with the combinations of six-foot and eight-foot sections needed to build the fence around the jumping arena. In the congress, the class constructed a combination chart. This is a convenient way to list all possibilities, but, more importantly, it can be used to explain earlier strategies such as the exchanges of equivalent amounts.

The Frog-Jumping Contest

The class investigates the results of a jumping contest in which they have to figure out the lengths of three frogs' jumps in order to determine the winner. The ideas of equivalence developed earlier can be used to solve for unknowns, and students use an open number line as a tool for thinking about the problem.

Day Six Outline

Developing the Context

☀ Introduce the three frogs investigation and ask students to work on the problems in Appendix I.

Supporting the Investigation

☀ Encourage students who might be struggling to consider drawing representations of the problem situation to use as a tool in their investigation.

Materials Needed

Three frogs poster

[If you do not have the full-color poster (available from Heinemann), you can use the smaller black-and-white version in Appendix H.]

The three frogs investigation (Appendix I)—one per pair of students

Drawing paper—several sheets per pair of students

Developing the Context

☀ Introduce the three frogs investigation and ask students to work on the problems in Appendix I.

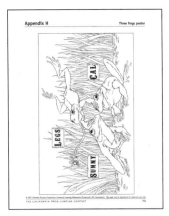

Explain that MT the frog has decided to hold a jumping contest now that the new tracks have been built. There are three frogs in this contest and the frog with the longest jump will win. Use the three frogs poster (or Appendix H) to introduce Sunny, Cal, and Legs. MT decides to change the rules a little for this contest: the frogs will complete multiple jumps; all the information taken together will determine the winner.

Distribute copies of Appendix I and some drawing paper to each pair of students. The appendix contains the results of the jumping contest. Have a short discussion with the class to make sure they understand the situation. The referee's frog-jumping rule applies: *Whenever a frog jumps in an event, if the frog takes more than one jump, all jumps are assumed to be equal in length and all steps are assumed to be equal in length.* However, different frogs have different-sized jumps, although the steps are the same. The problem is to figure out the size of each frog's jump. The frog with the longest (single) jump is the winner. Since some students will want to find the length of the entire jump sequences, this needs to be clarified.

Earlier in this unit, students used the idea of equivalences in order to prepare shopping lists for fences. Here, the idea of equivalence is again part of the problem context. For each frog, the two different jumping sequences are known to be equivalent even though the size of the jumps isn't known. In fact, it is the equivalence that provides the information necessary to solve the problem. This is a new way for students to use equivalence and so it is important to allow them time to make sense of the questions themselves. They don't know what the equivalent amounts are. This is a feature of solving for unknowns that students must become accustomed to. The jumping diagrams will provide a representation that will help them. For example, Sunny's data ($4j + 11 = 5j + 4$) can be represented on a track as follows:

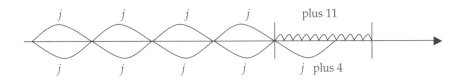

A representation like this is helpful in realizing that 11 steps are equivalent to a jump plus 4 steps. So the jump must be equal to 7 steps.

Do *not*, however, draw a diagram like this for your students initially. Just encourage students to draw the track and put on it what they know. As students draw these diagrams, they might encounter potential difficulties. They must pay careful attention to the words *forward* and *backward.* Then, the first time they draw equivalent jumping sequences, they may end up with different lengths. Cal's jumping pattern is tricky in this regard, because students need to align the two steps backward from the fourth jump with the six steps forward after the third jump. This means they may have to redraw the diagram. This redrawing process is very important; students need to know that the redrawing is not a mistake but part of the problem solving. For, initially, they don't know how big the jumps are, so they might not represent them as an appropriate length in their first attempt. *In fact, students should expect this to happen, because the lengths are the unknowns they are trying to find!* Once they do align the diagrams correctly, they should be able to merge them into one diagram. For example, in Cal's case, the first three jumps should align, and then the fourth jump should equal the six forward steps from the first sequence plus the two backward steps from the second sequence, showing that Cal's jumps are eight frog steps, one step bigger than Sunny's jump. The big idea of variation is involved here (j is a variable that is unknown, and it may vary until it is determined). As students redraw diagrams to represent different jump lengths, they are exploring variation—this redrawing process actually illustrates variation.

Supporting the Investigation

Observe the different strategies that students use. Some may guess and check, some will try to reason directly with the numbers, and others may draw diagrams. All the different strategies will be useful in the congress that follows on Day Seven, so allow students to take their own paths. However, if students encounter difficulties or if they have found jump sizes using numerical methods, encourage them to draw representations of the situation and use the diagrams as a tool for approaching the problem. Here are some of the strategies you are likely to see:

☀ Encourage students who might be struggling to consider drawing representations of the problem situation to use as a tool in their investigation.

✦ Guess-and-check reasoning using arithmetic. Students may just randomly try different numbers and do all the arithmetic until they find the size that works.
[See Figure 8]

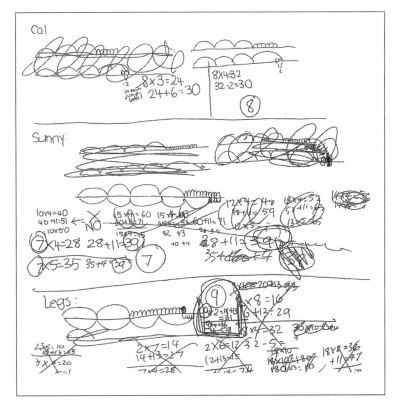

Figure 8

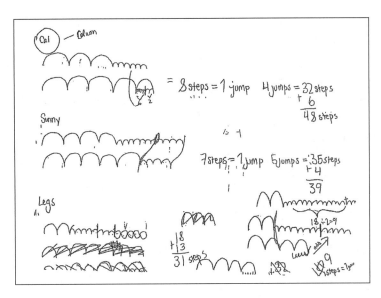

Figure 9

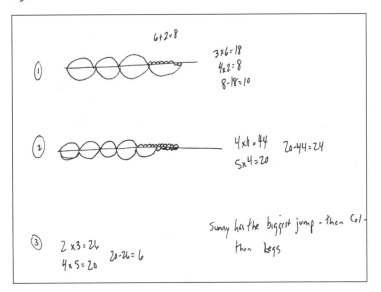

Figure 10

- ◆ Guess and check with adjustment. For example, in trying to determine Sunny's jump, students might try 5, get a result of 31 = 29, and notice that the left side is too big. They might try 10 next and get a result of 51 = 54, noticing that the right side is now too big. They may then reason (adjusting) that the size must be in between 5 and 10 in order to achieve balance.

- ◆ Most students will probably begin drawing the jumps on the tracks but will not align the information to make it equivalent. For example, they may use two different number lines and will not start the jumps at the same point. They might also make the error of not aligning the jumps. As you confer, remind students to use the referee's frog jumping rule and that both jumping sequences for each frog have the same length. *[See Figure 9]*

- ◆ Once students realize that the jumps must be aligned, that they are all equal, they will begin to make use of the equivalent pieces and separate off equal amounts. *[See Figure 10]*

The remainder of the class is devoted to this investigation. If necessary, students will have more time to work on Day Seven, after which they will prepare posters for a math congress.

Inside One Classroom

Conferring with Students at Work

Thomas: What if the jump is 10? Let's try that—4 × 10 is 40, plus 11 is 51.

Alyssa: I'll do the other one for Sunny. He has to land at the same place, right? 5 × 10 is 50, plus 4 is 54. Doesn't work…

Carlos (the teacher): Sometimes when mathematicians feel stuck they begin by modeling the problem. Have you thought of drawing the jumps and the steps, like on a track, or a number line?

continued on next page

Author's Notes

Thomas and Alyssa begin with trial and error using arithmetic.

Carlos acknowledges that mathematicians often feel perplexed. His remark helps students to realize that feeling stuck is OK and that modeling might help.

continued from previous page

Alyssa: How can we do that on a number line? We don't know what the size of the jump is!

Carlos: Can you draw the jumps on a track?

Thomas: I guess. *(Draws a track with 4 jumps and 11 little steps.)*

Alyssa: I'll do the other one. *(Draws a track with 5 jumps and 4 steps, but the tracks and jumps are now different sizes.)*

Carlos: It seems like your jumps and your track are bigger than the ones Thomas made. Does that matter?

Carlos does not tell the students to make the jumps and the tracks the same size. Instead he asks if it matters. Such questions help students reflect on important aspects of the problem.

Thomas: Yeah. It's the same track and they have to land at the same spot! You have to make yours exactly like mine.

Carlos: Since it is the same track, maybe you should just draw one. You could put Sunny's first trial of 4 jumps and 11 steps on the top and the second trial of 5 jumps and 4 steps on the bottom. And you are right, Thomas...they have to land at the same place, right? *(Both students start drawing on the same track, each doing one side, but the jump sizes are still not the same.)* I thought you said the jump sizes were the same?

Carlos stays grounded in the context, encouraging the students to consider that the track is the same. He thus uses the context to support a double number line representation.

Thomas: Oh, yeah—the referee's frog-jumping rule. Let's start over.

Reflections on the Day

Today students began an investigation to find the lengths of frog jumps when two sequences of frog jumps and steps were equal. The frog-jumping contest provided a context for using the open number line as a tool for representing equivalent algebraic expressions resulting from frog jumps and steps. In drawing representations and then redrawing them as more information was gleaned, students grappled with variation.

The Frog-Jumping Contest

Materials Needed

Students' work from Day Six

Large chart paper—one sheet per pair of students

Sticky notes—one pad per student

Markers

The students finish their investigation of the jumping contest begun on Day Six. They make posters and hold a congress on their work.

Day Seven Outline

Preparing for the Math Congress

☀ Ask students to prepare posters of their work on Day Six.

☀ Conduct a gallery walk to give students a chance to review and comment on each other's posters.

Facilitating the Math Congress

☀ Facilitate a congress discussion focused on separating off equivalent amounts to simplify problems.

Preparing for the Math Congress

Begin math workshop by explaining that students will complete and review their work from Day Six and then prepare posters for a math congress. Some posters will show how they can use diagrams of the frog jumps to determine the lengths of each particular frog's jump, although some students may have used other methods. Put posters up and have a gallery walk for ten minutes.

☀ Ask students to prepare posters of their work on Day Six.

☀ Conduct a gallery walk to give students a chance to review and comment on each other's posters.

▦ Tips for Structuring the Math Congress

Rather than having students simply share the strategies they used, look for some big ideas to focus conversation on, such as lining up different jumping diagrams so they match or replacing the equivalences by simpler equivalences. For example, in the case of Sunny, the equivalence of 4 jumps and 11 steps with 5 jumps and 4 steps ($4j + 11 = 5j + 4$) can be replaced by the equivalence of 11 steps with 1 jump and 4 steps ($11 = j + 4$). In a typical algebra course this process is sometimes referred to as cancelation (because 4J is eliminated from both sides of the equation), but students may find a different way to conceptualize and describe it. Because of the context of frog jumping, students may be uncomfortable with terminology like "canceling" or "eliminating," instead preferring terminology like "separators" or "putting it in a storage box." This type of algebraic simplification will be the thrust of the congress.

Facilitating the Math Congress

Convene the students in a meeting area to discuss a few of the ideas on the posters.

☀ Facilitate a congress discussion focused on separating off equivalent amounts to simplify problems.

A Portion of the Math Congress

Inside One Classroom

Maria: I drew 3 jumps and 6 small steps, and another 3, I mean, 4 jumps take away 2 small steps. And I drew this line because I decided to ignore these 3 jumps. There are 3 jumps on both sides of the track so that part is the same...so now the 6 steps and the jump taking away the 2 steps were equal. So ...

Author's Notes

Maria is invited to present because her diagram for Cal's problem has a vertical bar to indicate the equivalence of the first three jumps. This representation will allow Carlos (the teacher) to focus discussion on elimination. In discussing her representation, Maria has difficulty in explaining her line showing where the three jumps in each diagram align, and she hesitates for a bit.

continued on next page

continued from previous page

Carlos (the teacher): Before you go any further, Maria, let's see if everyone understands what this bar is on your poster and what you mean by saying "that part is the same." Turn to your partner and talk about what this bar or line on Maria's diagram means. *(After a few minutes of pair talk, whole-group conversation resumes).* Alyssa?

Alyssa: I think it is kind of like a separator, because the 3 jumps on the top and the 3 jumps on the bottom both meet up. But we want to see how the 6 little steps and the big jump minus 2 steps meet up because it is supposed to end up in the same place. So really this is the part that matters. The other 3 jumps aren't so important because they are the same.

Carlos: Is that what you mean, Maria? You separated the stuff that doesn't matter so much?

Maria: Well, it isn't that it doesn't matter. It's just that they…you could tell that they automatically meet up and that you don't have to worry about that.

Carlos: You could tell they meet up because…

Maria: Because 3 jumps and 3 jumps are the same thing. So the other parts are the important ones to consider. Then we thought if these two are the same… *(Runs her finger up and down between the end of the 6 steps and the 2 steps backward.)* So the jump is 8.

Carlos: So let me write what I think you are saying, so that we can all consider it. *(Writes:)*

$$3j + 6 = 4j - 2$$

This is what is on your picture, and you are saying we can separate out 3J from each and that means we only have to look at what is left, this part? *(Writes:)*

$$6 = j - 2$$

To give Maria some think time, Carlos uses pair talk so students can consider the issue Maria is trying to explain. She is describing the equivalence of the three jumps and the resulting simplified equivalence. This is a big idea in this congress.

Alyssa invents her own terminology and calls the line a "separator."

Carlos paraphrases what Alyssa said and brings Maria back into the conversation. He continues to clarify and to encourage the class to consider the representation and the equivalent pieces that can be eliminated—at least momentarily—to simplify the problem.

Carlos introduces the formal notation only after students have used the representation to discuss equivalence.

▦ Assessment Tips

After the math congress, jot down comments on sticky notes about the big ideas you heard individual students express clearly and the strategies they used. Place these on the students' recording sheets along with any other anecdotal notes and put the sheets in the students' portfolios. You might find it helpful to make a copy of the graphic of the landscape of learning provided in the overview of this unit (page 14). As you continue with the unit, you can shade in the big ideas and strategies you see students developing. Make one for each student's portfolio and map out the journey—the pathways—each student is making.

Reflections on the Day

Today students continued to explore the strategy of using equivalent amounts to simplify problems. Instead of "canceling" equal amounts, as is usually done in high school algebra, these students "separate" a problem into equivalent pieces. This separation is represented on a number line or with double number lines where jumps of equal unknown amounts are aligned.

DAY EIGHT
The Olympics

Materials Needed

The Pairs Competition (Appendix J)—one per pair of students

Hitting the Mark (Appendix K)—one per pair of students

The Toads' Three-jump, Two-step Event (Appendix L)— one per pair of students

Drawing paper—several sheets per pair of students

Large chart paper—one sheet per pair of students

Large chart pad and easel

Markers

The day begins with a minilesson that focuses on representations of unknown amounts on a number line. The class then investigates a series of problems involving frog jumps. These problems come from different events in the frog-jumping Olympics. Each problem can be solved by representing equivalent amounts on an open number line. Some students may begin to use more formal algebraic notation, including variables, to represent the problems. Work on these problems will continue on Day Nine.

Day Eight Outline

Minilesson: Representing Variables on a Number Line

☀ Conduct a minilesson focused on representing unknown amounts on a number line and developing the proper use of variables.

Developing the Context

☀ Introduce the Frog Olympics investigation and ask students to work on the problems in Appendixes J, K, and L.

Supporting the Investigation

☀ As students investigate The Pairs Competition problems, encourage them to draw diagrams of what they know and to look for relationships between the jump lengths.

☀ Encourage students to write equations to represent the problems in the Hitting the Mark and Three-jump, Two-step investigations.

Minilesson: Representing Variables on a Number Line
(10–15 minutes)

This minilesson uses a string of related problems designed to encourage students to continue using the open number line to represent algebraic problems. The string also develops the proper use of variables. Students should have a sheet of paper and draw representations as they go through the string.

☀ Conduct a minilesson focused on representing unknown amounts on a number line and developing the proper use of variables.

String of related questions:

Here is an unknown amount on a number line. I call it j.

Where is 2 times j?

Where is 2 times these 2 js?

Where is $4j + 6$?

Where is $4j - 6$?

Suppose I tell you that $4j - 6$ is the same as $2j$.

What now?

How about $2j - 3$? Where is it? Why?

What if I told you that $4j - 6$ is the same as $3j$.

What now?

Now where is $2j - 3$? Why?

Behind the Numbers

The string is crafted to encourage students to represent algebraic expressions in relation to other related algebraic expressions and to treat variables with variation. In the first problem, j is represented and $2j$ would just be twice it. The next problem will probably also be easy for the students. Now there are four equal jumps. The third problem introduces $+6$ and the fourth -6 and students may begin to comment that they don't know how big the jump is in relation to the steps. That is true, and such comments should be encouraged. Nevertheless, ask students to draw what the question indicates and share a variety of representations. Their diverse representations will promote discussion of this unknown quantity, since the size of the jump could vary. The next problem introduces an equivalent expression that may be a surprise and could cause students to have to redraw. As the string continues, new equivalents are introduced, causing further adjustments.

A Portion of the Minilesson

Inside One Classroom

Carlos (the teacher)**:** Rosie, show us where 2 times these two js would be. *(Rosie draws two more jumps. Now there are four.)*

Carlos: Does everyone agree? *(Several comments indicate agreement.)* OK. So here's the next one. Where would $4j - 6$ be?

Heidi: You take 4—no, I mean 6 little steps back.

Juan: But how little?

Author's Notes

Carlos has drawn the number line without any lengths indicated on it—starting only with one jump with a j above it. Now this original jump is followed by three more equivalent jumps.

continued on next page

continued from previous page

Carlos: Good question. How little?

Heidi: I don't know exactly. I just know that they're smaller than frog jumps. *(Puts little steps on the diagram.)*

Juan: But maybe the jump is smaller even than 6 steps.

Sam: Or maybe the jump is really big, like 100!

Carlos: You're right. We don't know what *j* is, do we? Well, suppose I tell you that $4j - 6$ is the same as $2j$.

Thomas: You tricked Heidi!

Carlos: I don't think so. Heidi didn't know the new information, so her diagram is correct for what we had then. What do we do now? Talk to your neighbor a bit about this.

Heidi: If $4j - 6$ is equal to $2j$, then that means 2 jumps are equal to 6!

Juan: Here's how Tony and I fit them together. I think we have *j* equals 3 now!

By asking "How little?" Carlos gets the class to reflect on the relationship between the size of the unknown amount and the length of one. (In fact, there is no relationship yet.)

Heidi has trouble answering an ambiguous question. The relationship is not known. But the representation can still capture the essence of $4j - 6$ and her diagram does it.

With the additional information, the representation Heidi drew has to be modified. This redrawing reflects the nature of a variable and this type of representation. The students have seen this type of thing before, and the pair talk here allows them to revisit this big idea.

Juan and Tony have found the link and they are able to use the representation to see that the information forces j = 3.

Developing the Context

☀ Introduce the Frog Olympics investigation and ask students to work on the problems in Appendixes J, K, and L.

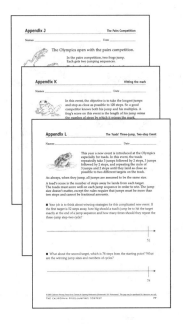

Tell the class that the famous jumping frog MT has decided to host the Olympics of frog jumping—not just a local contest. Explain that since the students have been so helpful in determining lengths of frog jumps, they have been invited to serve as referees of the competition. Not only will they be finding the jump lengths of many of the contestants, they will also be responsible for developing new strategies for efficiently calculating these lengths. By working on a variety of problems, some more challenging than others, and recording their strategies, the class will set standards for judging frog-jumping competitions. This work will continue on Day Nine. At the end of Day Nine, a math congress will be held.

Three sets of problems are available for the next few days. It is not necessary that all students do all the problems. A variety is provided as a challenge and as a culmination of the unit. If you are working with fourth-grade students, you may want them to do only The Pairs Competition (Appendix J) and then have a math congress on Day Nine. If you are working with fifth or sixth graders and you want to offer greater challenges and options for differentiation, you may want to break the class up into three groups. One group can work on the pairs competition, a second group can work on Hitting the Mark (Appendix K), and a third group can work on The Toads' Three-jump, Two-step Event (Appendix L). If students finish one problem, they can choose to work on another. It is also possible to begin with everyone doing the pairs competition, have a brief congress on it, and then work on the other two problems on Day Nine.

Supporting the Investigation

The pairs competition problems (Appendix J) require students to use various tools they have been learning about in this unit. Each problem can be represented on a number line and solved by fitting together unknown jumps. Solving them with guess and check would be difficult, although not impossible. The problems are designed to invite differing strategies. Don't prescribe any method; just encourage students to draw a diagram of what they know and to look for relationships between the jump lengths. In the latter two problems, students will probably have to find the length of each jump, but in the first problem they may not have to since they can find the amount they seek by comparing the two sequences. In the second problem, the increase in Smiley's jumps is a clue to the length of his jumps, and the proportional three-to-four relationship between Hopper's and Skipper's jumps provides a nice way to simplify the third problem. Encourage students to keep track of the different strategies they used. *[See Figures 11a–d]*

☀ As students investigate The Pairs Competition problems, encourage them to draw diagrams of what they know and to look for relationships between the jump lengths.

☀ Encourage students to write equations to represent the problems in the Hitting the Mark and Three-jump, Two-step investigations.

Figure 11a

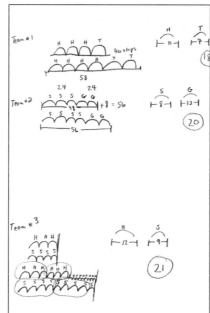

Figure 11b

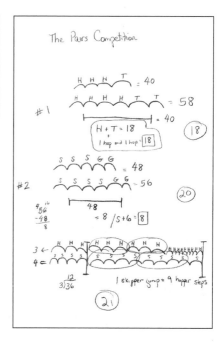

Figure 11c

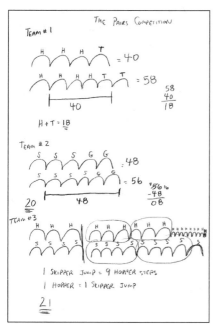

Figure 11d

It is also possible (if they haven't already begun doing so) that students will now start symbolizing with letters as variables instead of representing lengths on a number line. This, of course, is what they will do in some later algebra course. In using this strategy, students need to distinguish between the number of jumps and the lengths of jumps. For example, if they represent the first problem as $3h + t = 40$ and $4h + 2t = 58$, then it is important to discuss with them what h and t represent. Here h represents the length of Huck's jump and t represents the length of Tom's jump. The distinction and relationship between numbers of jumps and sizes of jumps were the focus of the congress on Day Eight. Note that during the next two class periods several minilessons are designed to help students construct this idea of symbolizing. However, it is not the goal to push symbolizing at this point as these problems suggest important strategies that can be represented in a variety of ways. Expect a diversity of approaches in the class, and celebrate them all!

The Hitting the Mark investigation (Appendix K) requires single variable representations. For example, Gauss' jumps could be represented as $5j = 120$. Archimedes' jumps would be $4j = 120 - 8$. The number line is drawn on the recording sheet to encourage students to use it as a tool in solving the problem, since students are not likely to begin with an equation. Once the problems are solved, you can encourage students to write equations to represent the problems.

The toads' three-jump, two-step event (Appendix L) pushes students to think about multiples of the expression $3j + 2$. In the minilesson, the relationship between $4j - 6$ and $2j - 3$ came up, and here students will need a different approach. Rather than halving the expression, they need to find multiples of it. In the context of this problem, the toads repeatedly complete cycles of 3 jumps and 2 steps, each time adding another $3j + 2$. For example, if a toad completes two cycles, this would be symbolized as $2(3j + 2)$, that is, $6j + 4$, or if they completed 5 cycles, that would be $5(3j + 2)$ or $15j + 10$. The objective is to land on a target and students are supposed to find the number of cycles and possible jump lengths that can work. For example, to travel a length of 52, students might first try to solve $3j + 2 = 52$, and when they cannot find an appropriate jump length (as $j = 16\frac{2}{3}$ isn't allowed), then they might next try $6j + 4 = 52$, which they can solve with $j = 8$. This is a solution because 6 jumps of 8 plus 4 lands right on the target—52. These problems will require students to solve various equations involving these multiples of $3j + 2$. This can be done on the representation, but those students who have begun to symbolize with equations will note the utility of working with such expressions.

Reflections on the Day

Today students began work on a sequence of problems requiring them to find lengths of jumps in the frog-jumping Olympics. The representations they developed will prepare them for more formal symbolizing in algebra, and different students will be in different places on the algebra landscape. It is possible that not all students will have had time to investigate all the problems. Students will continue to work on these problems on Day Nine.

DAY NINE

More Olympics

Students continue to investigate a variety of problems involving the Olympics context that was introduced on Day Eight and prepare posters for a math congress.

Day Nine Outline

Supporting the Investigation

☀ Give students time to complete the investigations introduced on Day Eight.

Preparing for the Math Congress

☀ Ask students to make posters of their work on at least one of the investigations.

☀ Conduct a gallery walk, allowing extra time for students to work on investigations they hadn't previously tried.

☀ Distribute Appendix M and ask students to work individually to record the strategies they have used, or seen their classmates use, for this investigation.

Facilitating the Math Congress

☀ Plan for a congress discussion that will highlight a range of student strategies for solving the problems, including the more abstract representations some students may have developed.

Materials Needed

Students' work from Day Eight

The Pairs Competition (Appendix J)—one per pair of students

Hitting the Mark (Appendix K)—one per pair of students

The Toads' Three-jump, Two-step Event (Appendix L)—one per pair of students

Student recording sheet for Olympic judging strategies (Appendix M)— one per student

Large chart paper—one sheet per pair of students

Sticky notes—one small pad per student

Markers

Supporting the Investigation

☀ Give students time to complete the investigations introduced on Day Eight.

As necessary, students continue the three investigations from Day Eight. These problems were discussed in the Day Eight notes (page 58). Students will develop various levels of representations, and some may use variables in their work.

Preparing for the Math Congress

☀ Ask students to make posters of their work on at least one of the investigations.

☀ Conduct a gallery walk, allowing extra time for students to work on investigations they hadn't previously tried.

☀ Distribute Appendix M and ask students to work individually to record the strategies they have used, or seen their classmates use, for this investigation.

Have students prepare posters for at least one of the Olympic events and display them for a gallery walk. If you have had three groups working on different problems, you might want to set up the gallery walk as a fair, with one table or "booth" for each event, and spend much more time on the gallery walk than usual. Supply extra recording sheets, paper, and markers at each booth so students can try the problems they have not yet done. Ask students who have solved the problems and made the posters to explain how the rules for their event work.

As students visit each booth and discuss the strategies, listen for important math ideas that you might want to have a class discussion about later. Remember there are two goals at this point in the unit. First is the continuing use of equivalence to simplify the questions. Whether or not students use symbolic notation, be sure to discuss with them how to express their strategies to record on their posters. A second goal is for students to construct more abstract representations for the problems. Some students may rely on the open number line, some may blend the open number line with symbolic expressions, and some students may be symbolizing entirely. During the math congress, you will want to have a conversation about how these different forms of representing the problem are related and how the same strategy can be represented in different ways.

After allowing a sufficient amount of time for students to visit the three booths and work on the problems they had not previously tried, distribute a recording sheet (Appendix M) to each student and ask them to use what they've learned from their own work or from their classmates' posters to list a few strategies that might be helpful for referees to know and use in these Olympic Games.

Facilitating the Math Congress

☀ Plan for a congress discussion that will highlight a range of student strategies for solving the problems, including the more abstract representations some students may have developed.

The math congress today should not merely reiterate the sharing of strategies used. That would be redundant, considering the lengthy gallery walk that the class has just completed. Instead, use the congress to record a list of helpful strategies that the referees could use in the Olympics. Here are some suggestions you might anticipate that students will offer:

- Simplify the problem by separating the parts that are the same. For example, if one frog jumps four times and then takes eleven steps to get to the target, and on another day jumps five times and then takes four steps, separate the four jumps and just look at $11 = j + 4$.

- Look for equivalent pieces, like four jumps of one frog being equivalent to three jumps of another.

- Substitute equivalent pieces.

- Pictures help. Draw what you know as a way to start, especially number lines!

- Write an equation about what you know.

- Use multiples, or halve, or double to make the problem easier.

Reflections on the Day

Today students completed their work on the Olympics. At this point students are moving beyond the context and considering the representation as a tool for thinking about unknown amounts. Some students were writing expressions with variables as they worked on the frog-jumping Olympic investigations. Today's congress enabled students to reflect upon different ways of representing the problems, some rooted directly in the context and some using abstraction in the form of variables. In either case, the basic strategies work the same way on the number line and with the symbols. These rules can be posted on a strategy wall as helpful reminders for future work.

More Problems and Assessment

Materials Needed

Assessments (Appendix N)— one set per student

Drawing paper—several sheet per student

Large chart pad and easel

Markers

The day begins with a minilesson that continues the focus on representing unknown quantities, as on Day Eight. The rest of the time is devoted to a collection of problems that brings together the various algebraic strategies that students constructed during the past two weeks. The problems can be either completed by pairs of students or used as an individual assessment.

Day Ten Outline

Minilesson: Representing Variables on a Number Line

☀ Conduct a minilesson focused on representing unknown amounts on a number line.

Developing the Context

☀ Ask students to complete a series of assessments designed to highlight the strategies they have developed over the course of the unit.

Minilesson: Representing Variables on a Number Line

(10–15 minutes)

This mental math minilesson is similar to the minilesson used on Day Eight. It has been crafted to support students in thinking about algebraic expressions in relation to other expressions. Each of the variables *x, y, a,* and *b* used in the string is introduced on the number line. Then, in the rest of the string, students represent what is asked by using or modifying that original drawing.

☀ Conduct a minilesson focused on representing unknown amounts on a number line.

String of related questions:

If this is *x* and if this is *y*, where would

    $3x + y$ **be?**

How about $2x + 2y$?

What if I told you that $3x + y = 2x + 2y$.

    What do you have to do with your

    representation?

Suppose this is *a* and i told you that $2a = 3b$.

    Show this.

Would $4a = 9b$ work?

    How would you represent it?

What about $16a = 27b$?

    Could you draw it on the same diagram?

Let's look again at the diagram for $2a = 3b$.

    Suppose that $9b = 36$. Can I find *a*?

Behind the Numbers

The first problem introduces a representation for *x* and *y*. Draw *x* as a jump and *y* as a different-sized jump. At this point the sizes don't matter since *x* and *y* are variables and their values are unknown. As you progress through the string, you will be forcing their values. The third question pushes students to redraw and to eliminate the equivalent pieces. For example, if students line up the jumps on the number line, two jumps of *x* can be eliminated, leaving $x + y = 2y$. So $x = y$.

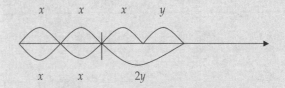

The next four problems are also related in order to encourage students to think about the relationships. The two problems that follow $2a = 3b$ are not consistent with $2a = 3b$ (in other words it is not possible to solve both $2a = b$ and $4a = 9b$ with the same pair of numbers *a* and *b*). A big idea is at play here: whatever you multiply one side of an equation by, you must also multiply the other side by, in order to maintain equality.

Developing the Context

Explain to the students that since this unit is nearing its end you have some problems for them to do individually so they can demonstrate all the wonderful strategies they have developed. Distribute the assessments (Appendix N). Ask students to do their best work so that the sheets can be put into their portfolios. If you prefer not to use these pages as an individual assessment, you can ask students to work together and use them as an investigation.

☀ Ask students to complete a series of assessments designed to highlight the strategies they have developed over the course of the unit.

▨ Assessment Tips

Ask students to use pens and to write in the work space provided. By requiring pens, you will be able to capture all the mathematizing—the false starts, the changes, even the mental work if only an answer is there. Although a correct answer with no explanation can occur from luck, this is extremely

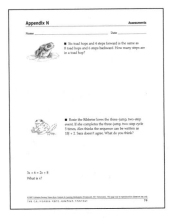

rare. Requiring pens and providing work space allows the thinking to be captured without requiring prose.

Make a class display—a sociohistorical wall—detailing the progression of the unit, an explanation of the important ideas constructed over the past two weeks using samples of students' posters, and a description of some of their strategies for determining how to arrange the benches and build the fence and to solve for unknown lengths of frog jumps. Display the combination chart as proof that the class found all the possibilities for fence arranging, and list all the wonderful strategies that the class constructed for referees of frog-jumping contests. By thus documenting all the elegant ideas and strategies constructed throughout the unit, you provide your students with the possibility of revisiting and reflecting on their work over and over again.

Reflections on the Unit

Sir James Jeans once wrote, "The essential fact is that all the pictures that science now draws of nature, and which alone seem capable of according with observational facts, are mathematical pictures" (Newman 1956) In this unit students were engaged in mathematizing frog-jumping contests (including bench and fence contexts). They modeled the situations mathematically with number lines, combination charts, and equations. Models alone are not very helpful unless they allow relationships to be explored with meaning. They should support the development of powerful strategies that can be generalized, and as the mathematician Samuel Karlin once said, "The purpose of models is not to fit the data but to sharpen the questions" (1983).

Throughout this unit students have been supported to develop mental representations using the number line for algebraic expressions. They have been encouraged to explore expressions as objects equivalent to other expressions and they developed important algebraic strategies such as substitution and canceling. Variables were introduced, allowing students to explore variation. All of these elements will form a strong foundation for the algebra they will do in later years.

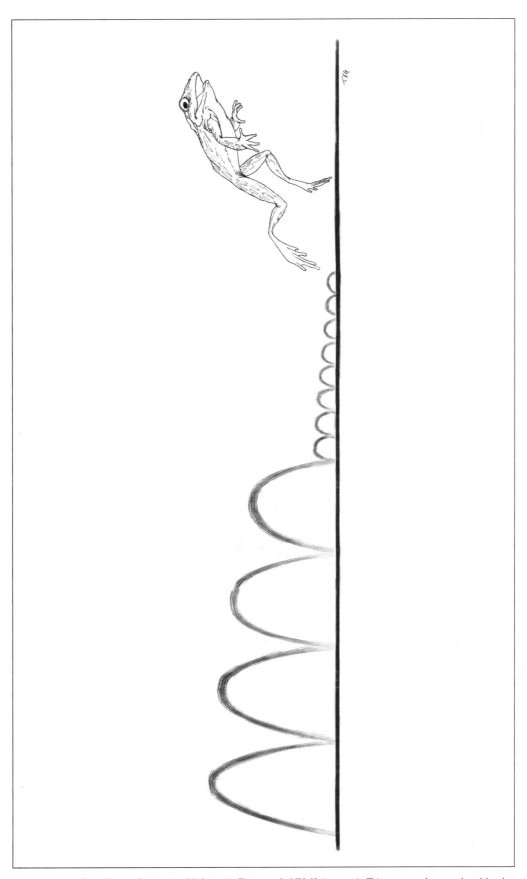

Names _____ Date _____

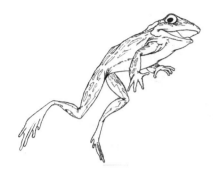

■ MT is a bullfrog. He is world-famous for his long jump. When he takes 4 jumps and 8 steps, it is the same as taking 52 steps. Use the referee's frog-jumping rule below to figure out the following:

1. How many steps are equal to 2 jumps and 4 steps made by MT?

2. How many steps are equal to each jump made by MT?

The Referee's Frog-Jumping Rule: *Whenever a frog jumps in an event, if the frog takes more than one jump, all jumps are assumed to be equal in length. All steps are also assumed to be equal in length.*

Names _____ Date _____

Frog's Jump Problem

Frog jumps 8 times. Every time he jumps, he travels the same distance. After 8 jumps, he has traveled 96 steps. How long are his jumps?

Toad's Jump Problem

It takes Toad the same amount of time to get to 96, but he does it differently. Each of his jumps is equal to 8 of Frog's steps. How many jumps does Toad make?

■ Represent both problems on one diagram showing jumping amounts, and explain how they are different and how they are similar.

■ **Marking the Meeting Points**

Where do Frog and Toad both land? Clearly, 96 is one answer. Are there other places where they both land?

Names _____ Date _____

You need to combine 6-foot and 8-foot benches to line both sides of two jumping tracks. The total bench lengths must line the track lengths exactly. One track is 28 feet and the other track is 42 feet.

- How many 6-foot benches and how many 8-foot benches are needed to line both tracks?

- Are there other possible choices of 6-foot and 8-foot benches that could be used?

```
┌─────────────────────────────────────────┐
└─────────────────────────────────────────┘
┌─────────────────────────────────────────┐
│                                         │
│          28-foot jumping track          │
│                                         │
└─────────────────────────────────────────┘
┌─────────────────────────────────────────┐
└─────────────────────────────────────────┘
```

```
┌───────────────────────────────────────────────┐
└───────────────────────────────────────────────┘
┌───────────────────────────────────────────────┐
│                                                │
│              42-foot jumping track             │
│                                                │
└───────────────────────────────────────────────┘
┌───────────────────────────────────────────────┐
└───────────────────────────────────────────────┘
```

- When the frogs went to the storeroom, they found that they had only 17 six-foot benches and 9 eight-foot benches. Will these amounts work? What should they do?

Names _____ Date _____

■ The frogs want to build a 52-foot-by-66-foot fence around their arena using pre-made 6-foot and 8-foot fence sections. Develop a shopping list of the possibilities for them to buy enough fence sections for all 4 sides.

66 feet

Jumping Arena

28-foot jumping track

42-foot jumping track

52 feet

Number of
8-foot
sections

8								
7								
6								
5								
4								
3								
2								
1								
0								
	0	1	2	3	4	5	6	7	8

Number of 6-foot sections

Names _____ Date _____

 MT decides to hold a jumping contest. The three contestants are Sunny, Cal, and Legs. In this contest, all of a frog's steps are the same size. Also, when a frog jumps, he always travels the same distance (the referee's frog-jumping rule applies). For the contest, each frog must complete two jump sequences and then take steps to end up in the same place. Your problem is to find out which frog has the longest jump.

■ **Sunny's Results:**

When Sunny jumps 4 times and takes 11 steps **forward**, he lands in the same place as when he jumps 5 times and takes 4 steps **forward**.

■ **Cal's Results:**

When Cal jumps 3 times and takes 6 steps **forward**, he lands in the same place as when he jumps 4 times and takes 2 steps **backward**.

■ **Legs' Results:**

When Legs jumps 2 times and takes 13 steps **forward**, he lands in the same place as when he jumps 4 times and takes 5 steps **backward**.

The Referee's Frog-Jumping Rule: *Whenever a frog jumps in an event, if the frog takes more than one jump, all jumps are assumed to be equal in length. All steps are also assumed to be equal in length.*

Names _____ Date _____

The Olympics open with the pairs competition.

In the pairs competition, two frogs jump. Each gets two jumping sequences.

The length of the jump for each frog is then determined and the lengths are added together for an overall result.

The winners are the pair with the longest combined jumping distance (one jump each).

■ **Team # 1:** Huck and Tom are jumping buddies. They decide to jump together and here is what happens: When Huck jumps three times and Tom jumps once, their total is 40 steps, but when Huck jumps four times and Tom jumps twice, their total is 58 steps.

■ **Team # 2:** Smiley and Grumpy won the competition four years ago. This year, their jumping totals are as follows: When Smiley jumps three times and Grumpy jumps twice, their total is 48 steps, but when Smiley jumps four times and Grumpy jumps twice, their total is 56 steps.

■ **Team #3:** Hopper and Skipper have a different technique than the other pairs. First Hopper takes three jumps and lands in the same place as Skipper does when he takes four jumps. Then Hopper takes six jumps and nine steps to land in the same place as Skipper does when he takes nine jumps.

Your job is to figure out which pair is the winner. When you combine the lengths of one jump for each frog in a pair, which pair has the greatest length?

Names _____ Date _____

In this event, the objective is to take the longest jumps and stop as close as possible to 120 steps. So a good competitor knows both his jump and his multiples. A frog's score on this event is the length of his jump *minus* the number of steps by which it misses the mark.

Gauss was the champion four years ago. He hit the mark exactly after 5 jumps and won with his score of 24.

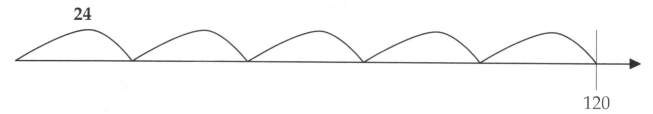

He beat Archimedes who in 4 spectacular leaps fell 8 steps short of the mark.

■ Find Archimedes' score.

■ This year's favorite to win is Newton and everyone thinks he can beat Gauss's score from four years ago. Close competitors are Pythagoras and Fermat. In 4 leaps Newton falls short of the mark by 4, in 5 leaps Pythagoras overshoots the mark by 5, and Fermat hits the mark exactly after 6 leaps. How large is each frog's jump and which frog wins the competition?

■ Make a poster showing the competition of Newton, Pythagoras, and Fermat.

Names _____ Date _____

This year a new event is introduced at the Olympics especially for toads. In this event, the toads repeatedly take 3 jumps followed by 2 steps, 3 jumps followed by 2 steps, and repeating the cycle of 3 jumps and 2 steps until they land as close as possible to two different targets on the track.

As always, when they jump, all jumps are assumed to be the same size.

A toad's score is the number of steps away he lands from each target. The toads must score well on each jump sequence in order to win. The jump size doesn't matter, except the rules require that jumps must be more than two steps and cannot be fractional amounts.

■ Your job is to think about winning strategies for this complicated new event. If the first target is 52 steps away, how big should a toad's jump be to hit the target exactly at the end of a jump sequence and how many times should they repeat the three-jump step-two cycle?

52

■ What about the second target, which is 78 steps from the starting point? What are the winning jump sizes and numbers of cycles?

78

Appendix M

Student recording sheet for Olympic judging strategies

Name _____ Date _____

■ Over the last two weeks you have been a referee for frog-jumping contests. You have had to figure out the size of many frogs' jumps and you helped to build benches and fences. What strategies did you develop—strategies that you think would be helpful for other referees to know?

Name _____ Date _____

Six toad hops and 4 steps forward is the same as 8 toad hops and 6 steps backward. How many steps are in a toad hop?

Rosie the Ribbeter loves the three-jump, two-step event. If she completes the three-jump, two-step cycle 5 times, Alex thinks the sequence can be written as $15j + 2$. Sara doesn't agree. What do you think?

$3x + 6 = 2x + 8$

What is x?